"Heather Dugan's book, *The Friendship Upgrade* is refreshingly real and witty. Dugan shares savvy wisdom and insight about how to build communities one relationship at a time and craft a life with meaning and purpose. I'm gifting it widely as a must-read for my friends and colleagues..."

—Caroline Dowd-Higgins Executive Director of Career and [illegible] Development, Indiana Univ[illegible]

"Heather Dugan brings a rare combination [illegible] experiences and exceptional communication skills to [illegible] This book will prove to be an excellent resource, not onl[illegible] [illegible]viduals hungry for meaningful connections but also for any organization that claims to care about people and the health and productivity of its work force."

—Dennis Hetzel, Executive Director, Ohio Newspaper Association, Columbus Ohio; President, Ohio Coalition for Open Government; award-winning author of *Killing the Curse* and *Season of Lies.*

"Divorce, an empty nest, a disconnected personal life; in *The Friendship Upgrade*, Heather Dugan nails the little secret that boomers never talk about... loneliness. Then she provides an action plan for creating a personal community to provide the connection and fulfillment that we all so desperately need."

—Donna Hull, Owner of *My Itchy Travel Feet, The Baby Boomer's Guide to Travel,* boomer travel expert at Humana's *My Well-Being* and PBS' *Next Avenue.*

"As an Executive in Human Resources, I find most of my professional energy spent on educating others about the nuances of meaningful relationship building. Most often, the primary impediment is a lack of self-awareness, but Heather Dugan has boiled that conundrum down in a way that anyone can understand and immediately begin to act upon. Plain and simple, this is a good read on both a personal and professional level for men and women alike."

—Jim McGannon, Vice President, Human Resources & Organizational Development at Sarnova

"As a mental health therapist, I can attest to the isolation women experience when going through different life transitions. Heather helps us 'feel' the painful emotions that come with isolation and a lack of strong women friendships. Thank you, Heather, for bringing this important issue to the forefront and steering women to take charge of their own destiny!"

—Shari Goldsmith LISW, Workplace Resilience owner

"Friendships are one of life's most precious gifts at any stage of life. Not only am I eagerly seeking them after reading this book, but I'm equipped to do it in a new way thanks to Heather who generously shares what she's learned in an uplifting and engaging way. This isn't just a book; it's a movement."

—Mary M. Byers, CAE, CSP, Author of *Race for Relevance: 5 Radical Changes for Associations* and *Making Work at Home Work: Successfully Growing a Business and a Family Under One Roof.*

"Heather Dugan put Cabernet Coaches together from an intuitive understanding that loneliness was a problem in all lives disconnected by divorce, job loss, relocation, or other common events in modern life. Her research-based understanding has grown through study, enabling her to write a high credibility book, but there is no substitute for the knowledge that comes with weekly sessions that have grown through word of mouth evangelism from women who've found Heather's outreach to be life changing."

—John Damschroder, News Producer, WKRC-TV; Columnist, USA Today Network

The FRIENDSHIP UPGRADE

Trade Clickable Connections for Friendships that Matter

Heather Dugan

Headline Books, Inc.
Terra Alta, WV

The Friendship Upgrade
Trade Clickable Connections for Friendships that Matter

by Heather Dugan

DISCLAIMER: Due to the sensitive nature of some of the content, names and identifying details have been changed as needed to protect the privacy of individuals. This book is not intended to be a substitute for the services of mental health professionals.

To order additional copies of this book or for book publishing information, or to contact the author:

Headline Books, Inc.
P.O. Box 52
Terra Alta, WV 26764
www.HeadlineBooks.com

Tel: 304-789-3001
Email: mybook@headlinebooks.com

Author photograph by Brenda Butler Kerns

Cover photo: Vacationing Cabernet Coaches friends Christine Williams, Francie Coner, and Molly Callahan.

ISBN 13: 9781946664570

Library of Congress Control Number: 2018962286

PRINTED IN THE UNITED STATES OF AMERICA

To those who still wait, wonder, and hope...

***

"The most terrible poverty is loneliness and the feeling of being unloved."

—Mother Teresa

"A friend is one of the nicest things you can have and one of the best things you can be."

—Winnie The Pooh

Foreword

If you knew me I would intimidate you. That's what I'm told. I run two companies. I speak in front of large groups. I train nationally in my field. I write articles for numerous publications. I hosted a national television show at age 24 and created/produced/and hosted a live radio show for three years because I had some white space on my calendar. And yet. In 2013 I sat in the parking lot of a restaurant looking through the plate glass window at a group of women laughing and talking. I was afraid to go in. I was afraid I had forgotten the skills I learned in kindergarten. *Can I make a friend?* I was overwhelmed by the insecurity of middle school. *Will they like me?* I was terrified at the possibility of being high-school-shunned. *Will I fit in?*

I was 53 and recently divorced. I had spent the past three decades in the tsunami of activity that is suburban life: children and sports, work and mortgages, driver's licenses, and SAT tests. All of which involve passing female acquaintances, but none of which give time for intimate connection with other women.

My children were grown, my career all consuming, my still-warm-in-the-grave-marriage isolating. I had no friends. Heather Dugan had been a guest on my radio show and invited me to her Wednesday night gathering "Cabernet Coaches"—a group of diverse women with one thing in common: a desire for connection. On that night in 2013, I got the courage to get out of my car and found a simpatico world of like-minded women. Like me, many of these women came to the group with far more baggage than will fit in the overhead. Each came with initial, tentative steps afraid that, like an old Polaroid, too much exposure would lead to a tossed away print. Instead I found a group of women who patterned acceptance and kindness after the woman that brought them to this mid-week respite; the woman who had the courage to go first. Heather Dugan.

As you will read in the book you are holding, Heather learned the need for friendship the hard way: through her own journey of brokenness, vulnerability, and yes, the "L-Word"—loneliness. The difference is she decided to go first. First into admission of need, first into causal analysis, first in creating a space for friendship; first in courage to invite others. The result is our Cabernet Coaches and the book you are holding: a time and place to exhale and admit intimacy is in our DNA. (And . . .while men are icing, women can truly be the cake.)

Read on. You'll read about me. You'll swear Heather knows you. She doesn't. She just had the courage to put in a book what we all know to be true: We need friends. Real friends with skin who will watch our dog. Deep connection. We need the Thelma to our Louise.

Pick up the tips (and the courage) to go find that friend. Invite a few more and go to dinner. Start your own Cabernet Coaches group. And while you're at it, go out in the parking lot and invite that woman looking in.

Kathy Chiero Greenzalis
CEO and Founder of Downsize America, LLC

Introduction

I didn't notice they were AWOL until a couple of years *after* I'd received the court-stamped "doesn't play well with others" ruling on my life. In fact, if you'd asked "pre-divorce" me, I'd have quickly but emphatically explained how busy I was with raising kids, caring for family, being a wife...Tactfully speaking—*Ahem. Would you just look at this schedule?*—there was *no* time for non-essentials. No time for diversionary detours.

"*Kids, we have to leave in five minutes! Everyone hear me? Five minutes!*"
I was married.
"*I don't care if Zak isn't in the car yet. Somebody has to get in the car!*"
Had found my life partner, created three beautiful children . . .
"*Who threw up? OK. Everyone,* ***out*** *of the car!*"
And was way past the need for women friends.

Unless you happen to be driving toward the Westerville Athletic Complex on Tuesdays and Thursdays around 4:30. Or in the opposite direction around 6. I can be flexible.

Like many of you, I'd kept saying "yes" to obligations and responsibilities until finding complete efficiency was mandatory to keeping a *most precarious* balance. I was great at meeting the needs of others but couldn't have envisioned meeting any of my own beyond an easy dinner that would feed five.

And then came the divorce, at which point a challenging two-parent schedule became mine to manage all by myself.

My new main objective at school meetings—besides sitting on my hands lest I accidentally volunteer to organize Teacher Appreciation Day—became scoping out the carpool options for the Mom Commute. Women were now essential because they tended to zip around in large minivans and SUVs just like me, and even the married ones could appreciate a good driving schedule.

My schedule flipped crazily between exhausting binges of activity and startling stillness with all of the living jammed into my "kid" days.

It was as if an invisible finger were toggling an on/off switch.

"On" held vestiges of my old life and meant time spent with my precious children. "Off" was filled with regret, guilt, and quiet desperation. The holes of these days were patched by day-long bike rides, visits to my failing grandmothers, frenetic work on my house and career…as meager hope leaked away.

"Off" was an increasingly heavy and sad state of exhaustion. I'd off-roaded my way from a comfortable country club life into the rough—a vast, prickly expanse stripped of any helpful guiding markers. I had said "no" to one life without choosing the next. And upon arrival, it appeared to be an empty neighborhood.

Oops.

I longed for connection on my isolated days but visualized it as a new and better man who would rub my feet and call me by name. It felt like I hadn't heard my own name in years.

Women friends *would* be very useful for meeting those eligible foot-rubbing men, or so it had seemed. In my regular perusals of local activities—the popular weekend festivals, concerts, and events—I often wished I had the requisite friends that would allow me to orbit in that alternate, more social universe. But it was a little late for that now, wasn't it?

Should have thought about that before you deleted the emails about new book clubs and moms' groups, you know, back when you were too busy to breathe.

Everyone I knew *now* was busy being married. Or, like me, struggling to manage an unmanageable life. It seemed my lack of forethought would leave me stuck on the sidelines—forever relegated to a "should invite" on holiday dinner guest lists, where I'd be teased with tales of somebody's great single brother only to be forgotten once I'd shivered my way home to an empty house.

"*What was that divorced lady's name again? Megan? Melinda? She was somebody's sister's cousin or something.*"

"Friend of a friend, I think. Say, did you get that marinade recipe? We should do those ribs when your parents come next weekend."

Finally, I posted an online dating profile. It made more sense than joining a bunch of clubs I wasn't interested in. Especially to my youngest sister and brother-in-law, who were finding me in their kitchen more and more on the nights my kids were with their dad. Yes, an internet "Hail Mary" felt a little desperate—kind of a barefaced acknowledgement of my social rejection—but maybe my new boyfriend would be social and have a lot of extra friends?

Although, once we were in love, the friends would be kind of pointless.

Don't hate me. You have to be honest to get to "real."

***

Two two-year-long relationships later, still *more* revelation. I had one of those soup-stirring "this needs something" moments. My life seemed to be missing some essential, foundational building blocks. Yes, a long-term love would be life enhancing, but before I could find "Him," maybe I needed to discover "Her."

Me.

Whoa.

Focusing on myself, absent a testosterone-framed context, was bold. Frankly, it felt like overkill.

Can't I just find a man and get on with it?

But now, as I look back—it was pivotal.

One of the big reveals, shared in my book *Date Like a Grownup: Anecdotes, Admissions of Guilt & Advice Between Friends,* was the negative impact of isolation on my dating choices.

"Loneliness makes fools of us all."[1]

Defining the cause and effect of my loneliness would prove crucial to life-changing intentional growth, my relationship readiness, *and* my re-launch into life.

It became clear that I needed to understand my own passions and pitfalls, my strengths and deficits...*before* I could ever begin to fit myself into a healthy romantic relationship. So, I embarked on some overdue therapy and self-reflection. It seemed important that I get happy about hanging out with *me.*

Otherwise it was like I was in sales without knowledge of the actual product.

As I learned and began to make some fundamental changes, it got better. A *lot* better! I found it easier to reach out to others when my world no longer spun backward and forward on their "yesses" and "noes," and I began to understand that there were a whole bunch of other women who felt like me on the inside—overwhelmed, lonely, and forever waiting for that magical, outstretched hand.

I found purpose in having female friendships, with no ambitions for anything beyond simple connection and perspective building.

Instead of being admission tickets to where I might meet a "life-fulfilling" man, my newly prioritized friendships became the main event. You see, as I developed authentic connections that enabled me to grow into the "best self" I envisioned, these friend connections grew to be primary. Female friendships trumped my hunt for love.

I began choosing friend time over bad first dates.

This was *not* a loss of romantic hopes! Not at all. It was, instead, a grasping of new possibility—an understanding that I could grow into "me" all by myself. With a little help from my friends.[2]

And it was this healthy, temporary detachment from my hunt for love—and the reattachment of *me* to *Heather*—that allowed me to solidify purpose and self and then ultimately open the curtain to genuine romantic love. Ironic, huh?

An alignment of purpose, proactive choice, *and* the realization that my challenges were actually opportunities for brand new achievements, along with an energized drive to create connection in my life, triggered a launch into my best decade yet. *And yes, I'm over 40. Um, OK, over 50 too. That's close enough, ladies.*

But let me start at the beginning. Because it really is a beginning to something better.

Friendships That Matter: My Cabernet Coaches

Platonic friends represent a valuation of our intellect and heart. There's no lust for booty or bounty. It's a primitive and yet often highly evolved connection—a wiring that esteems our core selves and then frees us to reach out and beyond.

Friend connections free us from the crush of loneliness and strengthen us to make best choices for ourselves—decisions that will be based not on deficits and needs, but rather upon opportunities and possibilities.

We need possibilities. And we need real invested friends, grownup friends, to help us find those possibilities within ourselves.

Friend-finding became my new treasure hunt. And these chosen connections, this eclectic group of random but like-minded women I found along the way, these are my Cabernet Coaches.

Quite typically, I didn't plan *any* of this, which should be great news for both the methodical *and* the organizationally challenged reader. Sometimes good things happen despite our best or least intentions. One small nudge for me became one giant momentum-building snowball down the mountain for womankind in my vicinity.

Observation: When hunger exists on a massive scale, people tend to congregate by the food table.

Did these women know they were special? Doubtful. There was no hint that we were even a group until Barb emailed that she'd created a repeating entry on her calendar. *More on her later.*

At which point, I thought, *Yes. We are!*

Since then, we've grown into a consistent, diverse gathering of women—at all ages and stages—united mainly by our simple desire to find and grow friendships. Nothing more, but nothing less either.

Cabernet Coaches is one of those eagerly proffered *"This is the BEST chocolate!"* revelations we're honor-bound to share when we find ourselves holding the plate. *"Who else wants to try something life-changing-ly wonderful?!"* But the origin of Cabernet Coaches, my DIY friend group, was somewhat random.

Six years after my divorce, I was once again a free agent after my unanticipated release from a two-year, hold-your-breath-and-swim-for-the-finish relationship that tanked badly at the start of a new year. The romance was a classic dead-end relationship, but at the time, I was committed to my commitment and had resolved to begin mouth-to-mouth once we got to January of the next year.

Instead, my back-burner boyfriend vanished. After I cycled through relief, despair, "What the hell?" and a little old-fashioned self-righteous indignation, I landed solidly in loneliness.

Can I get an echo in here?!

Slowly, I identified my need for female friends. Real face-to-face friends. After my divorce, I found I was sadly lacking these; I had no one to tell me my roots were glimmering or that my ex was over-reaching. The Cabernet Coaches group was my way of establishing change in my own life. I gave us a name and space on my calendar. And oh, how I hated doing that. I was much better with preferences and intentions than an actual commitment! But I did it.

Basically, I just started inviting people to hang out with me.

This required that I create a very general plan. And yes, in the beginning, there was a "What if nobody comes?" fear, but that dissipated fairly rapidly. Because, as it turns out, we were all looking for the same thing: Connection.

I've sifted through the old emails. Miles of "Hope you can join us!" and "Maybe next time!" missives that grew into "Can't wait! See you tonight!" messages. And I can see that it took time, a broader focus, and a bit of persistence. But I can see, very clearly, that it worked.

This Book

No. I have no way of knowing the unique set of circumstances that has enabled—or disabled—*your* capacity for forming lasting, life-enhancing friendships. I have no idea what life events may have torpedoed your original plan for this stage of life. In fact, all I can really surmise from here as I tap on my laptop keyboard is that your experience is likely to be unique and completely unexpected—*and that constant typing and elegant manicures are mutually exclusive. Dang.* How do I even know that much? From focused conversations with women just like you—and women who are, quite likely, different than you.

I've spoken with only children, eldest siblings, bottom of the pole, "hand-me-down wearing" youngest sisters as well as identical and fraternal twins... with women who have lived their whole lives within one zip code as well as women who moved almost yearly throughout childhood. I've interviewed married, divorced, and widowed women as well as lifelong singles. Moms of many, super-connected aunties, and those with a "no minors allowed" preference. Heterosexual, lesbian, and "I'm not sure." "In a relationship," "*always* in a relationship," "always in *search* of a relationship," and "I don't *need* or *want* a relationship." Women who, for many years, didn't care much for other females—who found themselves judged, viewed as competition, or undervalued. And yes, with women who, in the past, found other women to be petty, a bit of a time-suck, and a substantial energy drain.

Ouch. That hurts, doesn't it?

But I've also had long, energizing conversations with women who have found solid female friendship to be a transformative force now as they motor through their thirties, forties, fifties, and beyond. There are common emotions, trials, and takeaways—fascinating perspectives and fundamental truths—that thread our uncommon experiences.

"We need each other," said a friend as we recently finished lunch.

And indeed, we do. Not in an unhealthy, life preserver sort of way—but in the organically good capacity of illuminating grow lights.

In less flattering—*think "fluorescent-lit dressing room in January"*—under-the-bulb moments, these connections can feel like assaults against basic competencies and nit-picking diminishments to our overall self-confidence. But in the right light, female friendships help us to be our best selves—and better people than we dreamed we might be.

How can we help happiness happen when our pre-routed journey comes to an abrupt end, and how can genuine connection impact these life transitions?

What grows good *Cabernet Coach*-type friendships, and how can they enable us to explore and fulfill our deeper potential?

What qualities are common to healthy connections and what are the likely benefits?

Under what conditions are they more likely to occur and, conversely, what will deplete or doom them?

How can we find and nurture *Cabernet Coach*-type friendships, make them mutually beneficial, and tap into their transformative power?

Dare we ask about the ROI? We're busy. Is it really worth it to make time for female friends when we're role-spinning through motherhood, parent and grandparent care, career development, health maintenance and, maybe, hopefully, a marriage or love relationship?

I mean there are only so many hours in our overfilled days!

Let's find out.

Yep, I'm curious too. I've experienced the surprising impact of connection within my own life—a reverberating surge that has extended my launching steps far beyond my initial strides toward post-divorce growth. Solid connections that have helped me fortify resolve and act upon momentum-generating intention. I've developed a few quiet theories but want to understand and isolate any solid principles we can count on and build upon.

So, this will be *our* journey. Together.

SECTION ONE

Easy Avenues to Isolation

Take comfort in knowing that you aren't the only one living your life in a lonely bubble. Know that there are many other women floating in adjacent, disconnected spaces.

Chapter One

It's Not Just You

We're lonely. Not just you or me, and not just overachieving "*because* ***somebody's*** *gotta do it*" adult women. Like vines of climbing coiling kudzu, technology, mobility, weakened family ties, and our excessive efficiencies have combined to stifle genuine interpersonal connections around the world.

Once tied to the isolated elderly, loneliness has crept across age, social, and gender groups. It's an equal opportunity affliction interfering with the lives of the Greatest Generation and Baby Boomers on through the Gen Xers to the Millennials and Gen Z alike. In a 2016 Harris Poll of 2000 American adults, 72% of the respondents were familiar with that "lonely" feeling and 31% knew it very well, experiencing it at least once a week.[3] More than half of the 20,000 Americans surveyed in a 2018 Cigna study reported feeling alone some or all of the time.[4] Multiple studies in the UK, France, Canada, Australia, the US—virtually any developed country you might care to Google—recognize the negative impact[5] and growing concern over this pervasive societal condition. Over time, our civilized advancements have effectively decreased person-to-person sociability. The Oscar winners of 2008 can be readily accessed on any smart phone, but it's often harder to find a companion willing to share theater seats and a jumbo-sized bucket of popcorn.

We're paying a big price for our conveniences, and a myopic view leaves many of us placing the blame on perceived personal failings—which tends to squash any motivation to improve our social options. We're busy, exhausted, and tired of planning—*especially* us overcommitted, time-crunched adult women.

"By the time I get home from work and spend a little time with my family, there's nothing left," a young receptionist told me recently as coworkers nodded in agreement.

My weekly Cabernet Coaches gathering intrigued them.

"Can anyone come?" one asked. "I'd love something like that!"

It turns out that many *many* women would.

"Welcome to your Solo Suite. Your mega-media package with unlimited Wi-Fi will give you a great view of the much happier lives of complete strangers and

a skewed perception regarding your own problems, which look enormous, btw. Thanks for being a frequent guest! And of course, your blessings will also be included in the general warping at no additional charge. Um, double-checking our records...never mind, we'll ring your room if we find any."

It's alarmingly easy to check into Isolation but so much harder to leave. And—*Buyer Beware!* —it's a "no rewards" loyalty program.

And don't let that out-of-the-way ambiance fool you, there are *so* many routes to Isolation. Sometimes it's a steep cliff drop as with the "you get the friends, I get the dog" sort of disconnections that can occur after a divorce. Other paths are more circuitous. Perhaps a steady increase in work demands or the onset of an over-the-top and over-my-head commitment. "*Hate to be so 'last minute,' but can we reschedule lunch again? Maybe sometime after the spring fundraiser?*"

Only tax season or this quarter's marketing analysis will be followed by late nights helping with the school play, topped by a dishwasher leak, all to be trumped by somebody's unexpected surgery and the onset of the *next* quarter or season. Moms can easily be sucked into the ever-swirling vortex of our kids' needs. That strong "No" we perfected for checkout lane candy can be harder to access in response to the many developmental activities for the little darlings that come just a little later on. And it's the rare boss who will sympathize with your personal juggling. "*Yes, the reports are due next week, but I couldn't ask you to stay after 5! Go! Have a life! Reconnect with your family a while!*" *Yeah, right.*

Sometimes simple exhaustion leads to a fade-out. Other times, a heavier depression—triggered by the darkness of winter, grief, or a humiliating setback—drops a shroud that stifles motivation and depletes available energy, impacting our ability to maintain contact with the outside world.

We quit trying.

We lack the motivation and energy to reach out—and others quit reaching down to pull us up.

And then, we drift.

If any of this sounds familiar, take comfort in knowing that you aren't the only one living your life in a lonely bubble. How ever you got here, know that there are many other women floating in adjacent, disconnected spaces. Our increased mobility, valuation of efficient living, and a lessened focus on fundamental connection skills have left too many of us unconnected islands—more archipelago than community. We are now more vulnerable to the isolating impact of unfortunate career and financial events, divorce, death, chronic illness, and even positive life transitions that may disconnect us from an established framework.

Few of us willfully aim for a deserted island, but *isolation—and ensuing loneliness—can happen to any one of us!*

Unvarnished Disclosure: Lonely No More

Diane's effervescence rivals a sparkling wine—*and she could faithfully guide you to the perfect pairing for your health-enhancing entree.* You'd never guess she once had to choose between dinner and diapers.

Her early years were measured in bushels of apples and dozens of eggs. The family farm outside a small Ohio town filled most of her before- and after-school hours. Along with her two sisters, she tended horses, chickens, and an orchard. There wasn't much time for play or any friendships beyond the range of a bicycle.

But Diane remembers a single crystal-clear goal throughout childhood. "Even when I was three years old, my mom says I'd be hanging onto the pant leg of whatever man came into the room. I liked men. What I *really* wanted was a little attention from my dad. Always, and still...but my parents were screamers, and my dad was never an affectionate man. To this day, he can't say, 'I love you.' And I really, really wanted my dad to love me."

Like a *far* too obvious plot device, the family abruptly moved from their rural town of five hundred to downtown Los Angeles when Diane was sixteen. It's still a painful memory.

"It felt surreal. Dad got a big promotion. We moved into this apartment in downtown L.A. in the middle of January. Knew nobody. Couldn't go anywhere. Mom drove an hour to drop me off at this huge high school where nobody wanted a new friend. I was miserable. Gained thirty-five pounds in three months. Cried constantly.

"I still remember sitting in gym class on the very first day. The girls were talking about drugs and parties and sex—very explicitly. And I remember being just horrified and thinking, "*What have I gotten myself into?!*"

Diane hadn't gotten herself into anything, but she had landed in a very bad place, nonetheless, and would struggle for years to recover.

"Years later, I told my own kids, 'Be careful who your friends are. The bad kids will always take you in. They're non-judgmental because they really just don't care."

The partying crowd—more specifically the high school "kingpin" drug dealer—was her escape from total isolation. As Aaron's girlfriend, Diane had a place. But it wasn't much better than being alone.

"Everyone skipped class and got wasted. I didn't do drugs, but I drank a lot. Was absolutely miserable. I literally thought I was dying."

I asked about the other girls.

"They wanted nothing to do with me outside of the group."

And Aaron?

Diane shook her head. “It’s terrible, but I can’t remember a thing about him.”

The spiral continued. Her parents moved back to Ohio. Diane wobbled on, graduated from high school, and then worked as a waitress. The years that followed were drenched in isolation and spattered by bad relationship choices. Diane did whatever she could to make these liaisons work—because she had no Plan B.

At age 20, she landed back in Ohio, married to a man who abruptly left her for a 16-year old.

And Diane was pregnant.

“I begged my parents to let us live with them until my daughter was born. ‘I need help. I can’t do this on my own!’ Mom said, ‘It’s your bed. Go lay in it.’”

Somehow Diane did it—all of it. “There was no money for food. I lost a lot of weight. Worked a ton of overtime. Finally saw my way out with this guy I met at the company.” She laughed at herself. Rueful. “Yep, I just had to get my claws in him.”

There was another baby, marriage to a man she didn’t love and, eventually, heartbreaking sexual abuse of the oldest daughter by a family member. Diane worked three jobs to keep them all afloat. But when that marriage finally—thankfully—ended, she instinctively homed in on another man and began another painful relationship.

“He didn’t want me. Mike was happier by himself and should never have gotten married.” Diane poured herself into winning his attention just as she had tried with her dad. “I remember thinking ‘I need love so badly! If someone doesn’t fill up this vat I think I’ll just go crazy!’”

But again, it was to no avail.

There were some tears as Diane shared her hidden history—the distant details that shaped the woman who now sat in my kitchen, but her life is dramatically different now. “I’m very blessed.”

Diane is single. She would love to find the right guy, but she is very happy in her life as it currently stands. She credits her faith and the foundational connections she now has in her life—a couple of key friendships and our Cabernet Coaches group.

“I love Wednesdays! We’re just a whole bunch of women enjoying being together, catching up on whatever we’ve missed since the last time we got together.”

Actively building friendships made such an impact on Diane’s life that she often brings others who are fighting that shadow life of isolation. She now has enough friends and plans to fill any day or night of the week, but she remains forever sensitive to loneliness in others.

Isolation is *not* a measure of you. It's simply the default of a transitioning, overloaded society with more single adults than married couples. In *The Loneliness of America*, presidential speechwriter and author Janice Shaw Crouse observes that the people who would normally organize us into happy, connecting groups are no longer available[6]—they're commuting farther and working longer hours. *And scrolling through work emails on the sidelines of soccer games, hoping they remembered to plug in the crock pot.*

Loneliness *isn't* a character flaw or mark of disgrace. It's *supposed* to function as a signal—like hunger or thirst—that we need to fix something.[7] But when it catches us by surprise and we don't know what it means or how to deal with the sudden space, it's all too easy to wallflower one's way toward being an observer of life rather than an active participant.

No one's reaching out to you?

No one's reaching out to *anybody.*

Connection Point

I assume you're still holding this book because you felt a pang—an "I want that"—when you read the title, checked out the back cover, and thumbed through these first pages. And boy, do I understand! *In fact, I wish I were right there with you now, so I could say these words aloud.* Truly, it *isn't* just you. But you're the brave one looking for ways to make your life better. To shake things up and get connected with new friends—and that's WONDERFUL! *Please forgive a little all-caps enthusiasm there, because I really would be exclaiming (and embarrassing us both) if we were having an actual conversation.*

The first step is to release any shame you might feel. This isn't your fault. And even if you've been a steady contributor to the situation, forgive yourself already! Stockpiling shame does NOTHING for you! *Sorry for getting excited again, but this part is really important. And I really do care.*

Can you let it go? The embarrassment part? Put it in the category of an awkward stomach rumble during a client meeting or a child's badly-timed burp at a church service. It will be a lot easier to grow from here if you empty your hands *and heart* of stuff you don't need. *I have far better ideas for you to carry than that useless baggage.*

Think about this: Over one third, some 35 percent, of respondents to a national survey of adults over age forty-five reported personal loneliness.[8] That's one in *three* of all those people buzzing around you at the office, in the neighborhood, gym, or grocery store! That's every bronze medalist on an Olympic podium! So, this isn't really about you—although that's our immediate focus, for sure—this is about our society in general at this point in time.

So, you aren't so unique in this. Many others have a deep need for the same thing: Friendship. Connection. You're already part of a very large group—and it's time to plug in. So...can you just go ahead and let go of any embarrassment about feeling so isolated? It's temporary, like the flu. And now it's time to get better.

Connecting Thought:

A lot of people in my life, and maybe around me at this very moment, feel just as disconnected as I do. I'm not weird or defective—I'm just disconnected.

The bulk of present-day communication has morphed into a largely virtual experience wherein we can easily connect from an internet-cloaked distance and yet live alone in a crowd of neighbors.

Chapter Two

Opportunity Clutter

Remember how much time we were going to save with our smart phones and the internet? In the old days, *before* lunch was an Instagram share and we counted "special" with our senses rather than by how many likes it got on Facebook, communication required actual face time. Now, even those very words have been compressed and registered by Apple into an app that allows us to see faces from afar.

The Internet and smartphone technology promised us *more*—more time and more opportunity.

It certainly delivers on the opportunity end. Since the birth of the World Wide Web in 1989, we've experienced a steady increase of access to people and information. For instance, my best friend from kindergarten had *no* difficulty finding me here in Ohio from her home in Alaska via a quick Facebook search. As a side note, this increased opportunity to reach through time and space via the internet and social media has *sadly* been linked to marital difficulties in both the U.S. and abroad. In a 2011 study of divorce petitions in the UK, Facebook was cited in a full third of the filings[9] *—which makes Candy Crush look like a positive option in the land of diversions, huh?*—further underscoring how desperate our inherent need for connection can be.

Here's the thing: Information represents opportunity, but increased volume without consistent context and sort-ability leads to what I've been calling Opportunity Clutter.

***Opportunity Clutter:* An overabundance of disorganized and fluid options that can lead to pressurized inertia by extending the breadth and unwieldiness of decision factors while accelerating urgency, ultimately hindering actual decision-making.**

John Payne, a professor of business at Duke University, likens the Internet Age to a Dickensian "best of times, worst of times" scenario wherein the "wealth of information can lead to more confusion than clarity." Payne says, "the potential exists for us to enter an age of foolishness in decision-making, not an age of wisdom."[10]

Do you ever feel stuck in processing mode—with the spinning rainbow ball creating a fog of floating choices in your brain?

That's Opportunity Clutter.

In the beginning, it was easy to just add one more thing. And then another. And then—*Um, I guess we could maybe stack that over there*—yet another... *Go ahead! Pile it on!* We discovered multi-tasking and prided ourselves on our use of the simultaneous efficiencies unavailable to previous generations. With technological advancements, we could easily walk away from multiple in-progress tasks such as cooking dinner (*God bless the microwave!*), a conversation (the hanging text message), and even network and cable TV schedules, thanks to DVRs and Netflix. We could pivot between responsibilities with a simple shift of focus. It wasn't a big deal to juggle a group email over here, finalize dinner plans with a quick internet search over *there*, and do a little online banking and bill paying in between. But it's never that simple, is it?

(Looking up from laptop.) Ugh. The dishwasher is leaking again. Time to choose something more reliable. Cindy likes hers a lot. (Minimizes work email string and opens browser. Types Facebook message to Cindy.) Or is she still on vacation? (click, click, click) Wow. Great photos! Need to find out where they're staying. (click, click) OK. Back to the dishwasher. Guess I'll just ask for recommendations. (Post, reply, post, reply, post, reply . . .) Wow. Love Amy's renovation photos! Wonder where she bought those new countertops? (Private message to Amy who calls immediately). "Thanks Amy! Don't really have the budget to do the whole kitchen yet, but I'm saving the info! Just beautiful! Parent meeting? I'll have to check, but I think it's next Tuesday. Oh, Jim's calling. I'll let you know on the meeting." (Ring, ring, ring) Text to Jim—"Sorry I missed you! Dishwasher quit. (Sad face emoji) Eat out tonight? And then shop for dishwasher? (Heart emoji, praying hands emoji, smiley face emoji)" OK. Finish the department email, sort through the dishwasher recommendations, check on that parent meeting for Amy...(Reopens email.) Completely lost my train of thought. Need to read the whole thing from the beginning again. (Pause) Wonder why Jim hasn't texted back yet?

Sadly, we've completely overestimated our ability to mentally process so much at once! We're pretty perceptive when it comes to identifying distraction in others—*"Are you listening to me? What did I just say?"*—but we are rather generous in evaluating our own success. *Click. Click. "Uh huh...Mm hmmm." Scroll, scroll, click. "Would you mind repeating that?"* Unfortunately, it's now well-documented that the scattershot approach actually makes us *less* efficient *and* messes with all those brain cells that are still miraculously cooperating with us![11] It is simply too much.

We envisioned something more streamlined, slicing through all the excess like a sleek speedboat—*Quarterly sales report to the left, Mom and Dad's anniversary party to the right, straight down-the-middle cut through the homeowners' association meeting...DANG—The school play's tonight?! (Sputter,*

sputter, splat.) Yep. Instead of deftly zipping past the Miami International Boat Show crowd, we ended up in charge of an overloaded garbage barge, forlornly searching the coastlines for a quiet place to offload a lot of extra junk.

It's as if we have the key to a garage filled with everything needed to build one of those futuristic flying cars, but all the elements lie in a heap of disconnected parts, piled floor to ceiling, with instructions to be found—one sentence at a time (with assorted misspellings and grammatical errors, no doubt)—on scattered paper scraps. Simply *knowing* that building this vehicle will inordinately increase our wealth and enhance our lifestyle creates an ineffective urgency to complete an impossible task. We can't sort through it all, but the ready access obliges us to worry about the wasted opportunity.

According to Domo.com, we now collectively send 13 million text messages, filter through more than 100 million spam emails,[12] and obsess on weather updates more than 18 million times *per minute*—while we're undoubtedly multi-tasking to perform one of the 3.8 billion search queries Google receives *in the same sixty seconds*![13]

Forget the flying car—how about a recipe for the best grilled salmon as prepared by expert chefs, reviewed by your next-door neighbors and old high school classmates, and endorsed by patio grill manufacturers in cooperation with multiple purveyors of the "best" marinade?

Don't even think about adding asparagus. Who has that kind of time?

Exactly. "More time?" Not so much. In fact, we have *less* time for what we have traditionally valued—family and friends. With so many fast-flying opportunities, we've applied day-to-day efficiency beyond its intended use, often compressing our relationships to fit available calendar windows instead of creating the space to grow them well. More on the Efficiency Effect in the next chapter.

While the idea of online options was and is attractive to those separated by physical distance, the bulk of present-day communication has morphed into a largely virtual experience wherein we can easily connect from an internet-cloaked distance and yet live alone in a crowd of neighbors.

"Busy" is our standard response to "How are you?" and slow-cooked conversations have become the luxury meal.

Burdened with Benefits

Careers and/or motherhood forced many of us to fast forward past many of our choices—flashing through years at a time as we *managed* our schedules, *shuttled* our kids, and *squeezed* in the occasional date night with a spouse. Often, we began minimizing our engagement levels to maximize potential possibilities, shifting our focus from present moments toward the creation of memories to be enjoyed in the future.

If you were one of the "if it's Wednesday, it must be hockey" parents, your family may have struggled to get a quorum at the dinner table. Sad, but true. In recent years, the simple joys of family have frequently been overrun by a surge of good intentions and the ubiquitous opportunities to do more for our kids. While properly structured youth sports participation is linked to increased confidence, well-being, and self-discipline for the athlete, according to a Canadian study by *The International Journal of Environmental Research and Public Health*, the impact of intense sport commitment on the family unit as a whole can be detrimental.[14] Because sacrifices aren't limited to heroics on the field, and that trade-off can alter family dynamics and weaken cohesiveness. This same study cites the parental stresses inherent in adapting family routines to fit the practice, training, and competition demands of the sports and/or extracurricular activities of their children. Parents are often surprised by the increasing commitment of time and money but reluctant to scale back and pull the plug on a child's dream. So, the family takes the hit, scheduling holidays, finances, and sometimes even careers around their young athletes.

Not surprisingly, the bulk of the load often falls on Mom, supreme facilitator of Team Family. Already documented as spending an average of 72 additional minutes per day on household activities and caring for household members than fathers,[15] the added requirements of sports or other time-intensive kid commitments in the arts can lead women to sacrifice careers and social lives for the good of the team.

It's in our nature to nurture. But it can be very stressful and isolating for the one gathering shin guards, snacks, and carryout dinner after her 4:30 meeting.

No judgment from me. We were one of those families. Our kids loved soccer, track, cross-country, dance, swimming, drama, music, and more. For a parent, watching our children discover and develop their unique gifts can be one of life's great joys. But the balance is so tricky that it's hard for most of us to manage well. In the best cases, parents laugh at their own exhaustion and carve out space to maintain their equilibrium and one-to-one connection. For others, however, an intensive extracurricular schedule can trigger a repetitive drilling into existing fractures we haven't the time or energy to fix. My family's seasons of three, four, and even five simultaneous extracurricular activities made sense at the time, but in retrospect—there was a costly exchange of couple time and even self-identity for the development of our progeny's talent and enjoyment of sport and arts. Would I do it again? Some of it. But I would also say no more often. I would honor my own loving, maternal instincts more, and I would set boundaries that better established the supremacy of the family unit.

For most of us females, our midlife main entree will be dominated by some generous sides: a challenging career, parent or grandparent care, the responsibilities of home ownership, children's activities and all the normal auxiliary needs of a family, plus our own education and professional development. Too often, we mutate into a Treadmill Warrior. Can you picture her? In constant motion, she ignores the on-hold music emanating from her cell phone as she taps away at work deadlines on a laptop, keeping an alert ear for a microwave oven beep while assuring her eleven-year old daughter that life really is bigger than middle school.

"Really Mommy?"

"Yes, Sweetheart. Those girls aren't being good friends. You'll find better ones. I know this is such a hard time—I hated middle school—but it will get easier as you get older."

"Promise Mommy?"

(Sigh) "Yes, Sweetheart."

"Who are your friends, Mommy?"

Oh dear. I don't have time for this. And then the *save.* An "emergency" text message.

"Just a minute. I need to get this. Work."

Clickable Connections

In managing Opportunity Clutter, quicker, shorter connection points can become a seemingly essential timesaver.

"Sally? She's a 'Facebook friend.'"

In other words, "Don't ask me how she's doing. I haven't seen her in a bazillion years, if ever, and I know her only by what appears in my filtered newsfeed. Oh, and she takes a lot of selfies with her cat."

We have a lot of these—Facebook friends are the new collectible you don't have to dust. Practically maintenance-free, they *do* serve a useful social and entertainment purpose. They're often an effortless "people you may know" find, easy to attach without getting hooked into a future dinner invitation. *Add Friend? Click.* The ultimate in friendship efficiency. Nothing need be committed to memory or heart, as most of the salient items—birthdays, relationship status, life events—are saved for you as searchable reference points. *How convenient is that?!*

"Happy Birthday (*fill in the blank*)!"

A lively social media life can create an illusion of connection—*and, mercifully, you can even fine-tune and soft-focus that illusion with photo cropping and filtering apps.* But absent actual face-to-face contact, these can be more like an interactive video game than bona fide social interaction and can feel like a "possibility" pile-on. And while thoughtful, *active* engagement via social media can boost our sense of well-being, *passive* use has proven detrimental effects.[16]

Virtual interaction allows us to travel *around* connection with training wheels—wobbling along between likes and reposts with a quick comment here or there—but without real commitment. If left to live online, these friendships will rarely take off toward meaningful connection. If a contact's posts are too happy/sad/political/weird/*your choice here*, disengagement is but a click away.

We can "unfriend" as easily as we switch the evening's Netflix selection. While the sensitive may feel an emotional tweak should such an unfriending be noted, the ending of a social media "friendship" is usually a non-event—more of a discontinued item than cancellation of anything tangible.

Delete.

Through the reach of social media, we've gained a much bigger pond—but it's barely a splash pool, spread out to a depth that will barely dampen our souls. And we need to get our feet wet.

Even worse, virtual friends can begin to look like the Barbie dolls of our youth, either absurdly perfect with their "Malibu tans" and accessory-laden lives, or a little too exposed—cringe-worthy lessons on the long-term miseries of whim-driven living. *The unfortunate consequences of scissoring Barbie's hair—"No, it will* ***not*** *grow back!"—were pretty minor compared to the forever ramifications of rash, and potentially viral, online behavior!*

Clickable connections are convenient, somewhat entertaining and often better than nothing at all. But relegating primary interactions to the virtual leaves us more observer than active participant, and ultimately, clickable connections allow us to extend and perpetuate our isolation.

Unvarnished Disclosure: A Facebook Window on the World

"He was so critical and paranoid, I couldn't post much of anything myself. So, I just lurked, for the most part, watching everyone else's lives go by."

An ill-advised marriage to an alcoholic man turned abuser had restricted Ava's life to working two jobs and facilitating a home life for her two kids and the heavy drinker. "I'd get home after work and make dinner while he got drunk watching YouTube videos in the next room. Then we'd eat, listening to him bitch about how stupid everyone was. After dinner, he'd head right back to the sofa, leaving me with the dishes. I'd eventually go sit there beside him, watching whatever he put on for us. *That* was a typical Friday night."

As is typical of abusers, her husband actively worked to disconnect Ava from the life she'd known through physical and emotional intimidation and by demeaning all of Ava's friends and interests. He restricted her social life, fearing she'd reveal the ugly details about their miserable marriage. "No coffees; no lunches. It wasn't worth the anger and jealousy."

"Occasionally, I'd go on Facebook to watch the 'normal' lives of others: old friends going out and having fun, making social connections. Enjoying all the things I could no longer do."

I asked if seeing those so-called normal lives online ever motivated her to seek help in any way.

"Never. I was completely dead inside. The more I watched life go by, the more helpless and isolated I felt. There was no hope for me. I felt stuck, with no way out. It was too big a risk to my personal safety to even try. Facebook felt like looking through a window at the world, and even though I knew the lives I watched weren't all as perfect as they seemed, it was nowhere near the realm of my reality. *My* reality was a drunk who controlled almost every aspect of my life. I found out later that he even had a forward on my emails! He'd log onto my Facebook account to post incoherent, cryptic messages on my wall that I'd race to delete when he wasn't paying attention. He texted my daughter from my phone, pretending to be me, and would even call my *ex-husband* to *talk* about me! He took my life away."

A Christmas Day altercation and 911 call finally provided Ava an exit. She knew it was then or never and reached out to one of the few friends she'd been able to maintain any degree of contact with. Once the full truth was revealed, she found the support she needed to move her family to safety and file for civil protection and divorce while her husband was jailed.

Past the crisis, Ava is thankfully getting her life back on track now. Safe to make her own choices, she also feels more confident in her ability to make them. And while she finally has unrestricted, private use of her Facebook account, email, and cell phone, Ava also has a new awareness of the limits of virtual connection. The courage to end the misery of her isolated existence only grew with real human contact. Ava withered without it.

"Facebook showed me what I was missing, but I had to step around the veil."

Hoarding and Procrastination

The onslaught of opportunity can also make us hesitant to commit on yes and no decisions that absorb calendar space. *Why decide now when there may soon be something better?* There's a temptation to avoid active selection in favor of generating more choice, but this manner of postponement only increases the unwieldiness of any future decision. The string-along "maybe" or "interested" response offered by Facebook even allows us to change our mind with a gentle reverse. Granted, these generally aren't black tie, get-a-fresh-pedicure affairs, but this more casual attitude has invaded the social circuit, leaving would-be hosts with no options but to pad and subtract.

And have you noticed the boom in storage and organization solutions for our "more, more, more" state of mind? Sales of U.S. manufactured organizational products for the home grew at a rate of 3.5 percent between 2010 and 2014, a time when the national economy slumped along at less than half that rate, and retail sales for our "pack it and stack it" solutions are projected to reach a mind-boggling $19.5 billion by 2021.[17] Some of this stems from well-intended repurposing—we save baby clothes for the next sibling or hold onto family heirlooms for a next generation. But, it gets out of hand.

Often, an accumulation of *stuff* represents choices yet to be made. Sorting requires mental engagement—a dive into the depths of decision-making. Instead, we invest in bigger closet organization systems that allow us to file away our "maybe"s rather than donate them to someone who might actually use them. It's easier to stack boxes than to evaluate the contents, so we just keep all our "might need/want/use" items, bemoaning the clutter as we bury our "possibly want" items where we can't possibly find them.

We also do this with people.

I first noticed this troubling phenomenon during my research for *Date Like a Grownup.* While I heartily endorse the inclusion of digital dating as part of a concerted search for long-term love, many adult singles use this tool imeffectively—in a way that makes dating in perpetuity more likely than the oft-stated goal of finding and growing one healthy, monogamous love relationship.

In the online dating world, *Comparison Shoppers* are long-term data gatherers who never make an actual selection.[18] Bedazzled by the electronic array of potential partners, to be fine-tuned with a keyword here and a search option there, they succumb to the "Ding! Ding! Ding! Could-we-have-a-winner?!" adrenaline rush only to get overrun by the Opportunity Clutter found on dating websites and apps. The desire to investigate options is understandable and wise, but it's all too easy to begin shopping for "best available" and potential upgrades—never making the yes/no decisions that are essential to finding a "Right Fit" relationship.

The same behaviors can be observed at many networking events where business professionals trick or treat for contacts rather than engage in the opportunities for conversational connection. Similarly, Facebook and LinkedIn have grown from devices for connection into collections of contacts because *more* is always better. We may not *feel so* connected, but we sure like the look of "500+" on our LinkedIn profiles!

But just as a hoarder is usually unable to locate specific items, *we don't know where anyone is!* We gather because we don't want to leave anything behind. We're afraid we might need someone someday but are ill-equipped to do more than file them away for now. And knowing we have so many options—but so few real connective friendships—feels empty.

A networking hoarder will focus on tying knots—"*Hey, I'll find you on LinkedIn*" or "*Give me your card.*" A true connector is a weaver of people. She gathers in second-tier details and notes intersecting ideas. The hoarder plays a numbers' game and hopes to score big for a specific need. A committed connector, on the other hand, visualizes connection as a living tapestry that integrates, incorporates, and includes—as opposed to a simple web of linked contact points. This level of connection necessarily requires better focus, assimilation of information, and an interest in asking questions rather than simply sharing one's own story.

There are very few true connectors, professionally- and personally-speaking. A genuine "people person" stands out, doesn't she? Many of us aspire to be one, but over-efficiency, our less practiced skills, and the enormity of the challenge have relegated most to simply hoarding contacts instead of growing potential connections.

We have a lot of "She'd be a good friend" friends, don't we? Women we're pretty sure we would enjoy having a history with, but maybe at some future point when there's actually time to develop one.

Overfilling the Funnel

While Opportunity Clutter has increased the influx, overwhelming our lives with more than they can reasonably hold, the funnel of available time—through which all of it must flow—has narrowed considerably. Increased responsibilities in the form of aging parents, heightened economic constraints, and employment demands diminish our flexibility even as we grow our daily "essential" task lists.

We have less time to manage and appreciate *"But wait! There's more!"* add-ons, and the burgeoning stream of information, "would be nice" possibilities, and "don't forget"s have swelled far beyond the channel of usability.

Our cups runneth over—and *overwhelm-eth* us!

With*out* a funnel, I tend to spill candle oil onto countertops when I'm refilling the favored dinner lighting in my house. I'm reasonably coordinated—*totally have the whole "left, right, left, right" walking thing down*—but it's difficult to gauge the speed at which the marble-sized glass repository of my favorite wick burning candle will fill as I pour in the oil. Absent the plastic guidance of my kitchen funnel, refilling the oil well would simply be too much work. Even *with* a funnel-assist, I've created a few countertop oil slicks by overestimating the capacity of one that was simply too small for the job. I'm basically two spills away from simply dimming the overhead lights, and I *love* candlelight!

Most of us began adult life with a few empty rooms, metaphorically speaking. It was early within the living/accumulating process, and we still had some mental and physical latitude—unfurnished laboratory space—wherein we could fuel our aspirations. Yeah, that first job was big stuff, but there was also time to ponder our unknowable futures as we moped about our love lives and imperfect childhoods. We had time to get tired. To get bored. To grow motivation.

This might have changed—dramatically so—with the addition of a spouse, kids, and/or a more demanding career. As with spare bedrooms and closets or any one of our mega-gigabyte devices, over time we managed to fill any extra space. *Bye-bye breathing room.* Cramming in complications and time commitments, we displaced essential mental margins with miscellany, to the point that many of us now need de-stressing activities to enable disengagement. And we long for the simplicity of an unconstructed moment.

As more of life is structured around the demands of a family that may include both kids and aging parents and a career that requires some retention effort, unscheduled time shrinks dramatically. In recent years, this overfilling phenomenon has exploded, and as our capacity has been stretched beyond foreseen limits, our focus and patience have also diminished. And when "too much" rubs against "too little," it can spark a little stress...or even a lot of stress. We expect more and tolerate less as we race the loops between perceived emergencies and deadlines.

Compressed responsibilities leave many of us acting more like stressed administrators of our lives than happy participants.

One reasonable response to being overloaded and completely out of time might be to find some help. That's what mom did—*"Set the table if you want dinner!"*

Another valid option might be to cut something out, right? It's *amazingly* easy to slice and dice somebody *else's* excesses. Husbands can be great at this—*"You're too busy? Why do we need to clean the windows anyway?"* I've certainly tried that approach with a few friends—*"Do you have to actually bake the cookies for the banquet yourself? Can't you just rough-up some store-bought cookies a little?"* But our standards and expectations for ourselves can be pretty rigid.

Many of us have, in fact, further restricted that narrowing funnel of time with some ineffective customizations. Instead of choosing and channeling our most valued essential commitments across a slippery smooth surface, we inadvertently line our funnels with super absorbent sponge-y materials such as Guilt and Hyper-responsibility. Like martyr-maniacs, we tend to be more skilled at addition then subtraction, permitting history to become our default habit—*"Well, I guess if we did it last year."* We allow "should" unfettered access to our schedules.

On any given day, we have guilt options for just about every sector of living because choosing one thing *always* means letting go of another "priority." But the prospect of consciously releasing any *one* priority when *everything* is a "priority"—a class of event and commitment that seems to grow in volume *by the minute*—often *leads us unto procrastination.* Instead of doing an active edit on what goes into the funnel, we widen our arms and run faster (Remember Treadmill Woman?), telling ourselves everything will *somehow* fit when it's actually a physical impossibility. That's bad running form—bad *anything* form—and almost by default then, spillage happens. And very often, since our inner voice is never as loud as the chorus chanting, *"Can't you just do this one thing?"* the stuff that drips over the side, that puddle by the funnel, will likely contain the essentials to our own self-discovery and growth.

Connection Point

Are you a digital collector? It's much easier to spot our excesses when they're hanging in a bedroom closet or sitting on a bookshelf. *Strike the last one—you can never have too many books!* But for many of us, the worst, most anxiety-producing clutter is in our brains.

Brain clutter is a writer's worst nightmare. While streams of congruent ideas and alternative word choices are useful, there has to be some disciplined paddling through the paragraphs to stay on course. Personally, I'm susceptible to any and all distractions: piles of yet-to-be-folded laundry, stacks of bills, email notifications, text messages...

What's your weakness? Where is Opportunity Clutter preventing active choice? The first step to reprogramming any sort of bad habit is to identify what it is and how it's impacting your daily life. Is a Netflix binge watch your default on the weekend? Have you suggested, "We really need to get together!" to acquaintances multiple times but never managed to follow through? Maybe you continually find yourself scrolling through Facebook: Is there a purpose to the clicking, or are you simply doing the digital equivalent of snacking because you're bored? Identify where you're indefinitely stuck in gathering mode.

The second step is choosing your new action. Many days, I have to basically induce my own hibernation by turning off all computer notifications and hiding my phone as I cozy up to my laptop. I mentally box up non-relevant thoughts such as planning college visits for my son, lingering concerns for friends and family, and the realization that I *still* haven't changed the furnace filter. I even talk to myself—my spoken thought acting as a tether to the present moment and task. *CNN: Hey Heather! Check out this breaking news item, and while you're at it, check out these great destinations in Travel! Me (closing the browser): Save it for later, Heather. You're making great progress here. Get this done first.* This simple statement prompts me to disregard tempting distractions and make an active choice to write.

Selectivity is truly a mindset. I find the precedent of standing at my garage trash can with the day's mail—junk mail isn't allowed across the threshold—helps me be more methodical as I mass delete emails later. And as I move toward downsizing my housing with weekly household purges, it makes me more selective on what I buy or randomly keep. In interpersonal terms, I've grown better at discerning connective opportunities versus time-fillers. I prioritize appointments and events that facilitate conversation over small talk. And as an eligible adult single, no "first date" will *ever* trump time with my foundational friendships.

Connecting Thought:

I'm not needy—in fact, when I look at my (internet use/calendar/responsibilities/*fill in your own)*, maybe I've been gathering a bit *more* than I actually need. So today, I will try to select rather than collect. I will choose. This means I will say "no" and actually let go of a few options that I don't really need or want. How wonderful that I have more than I truly need and can instead begin choosing items, connections, and activities that will truly enhance my life!

We've adopted efficiency as a lifestyle instead of a temporary sacrifice.

Chapter Three

The Efficiency Effect

One of the first things to go, because it's "just" lunch or coffee or a catch-up conversation that can be rescheduled (*and rescheduled*), is Connection. With lives that often resemble the proverbial junk drawer—loaded with stuff that seems worth keeping simply because we're afraid to throw anything away—increasing the efficiency of our essential connections feels like a logical response to an illogical load.

But this leaves us with burgeoning contact lists and no one to talk to. Flying about between responsibilities and the ever-present diversions, we have full lives, often edging into Thanksgiving-dinner-stuffed lives during our busiest seasons. No one can argue this *or would even have the time to do so,* but *full* feels so-o empty—because the fillers are non-sustaining obligations and events.

We're chronicling our lives instead of living them. Trying to keep friends—*"Let's do coffee soon"*—instead of growing friendships. Our full lives feel empty because we're partaking of the meal, the feast of life, alone.

We've adopted efficiency as a lifestyle instead of a temporary sacrifice. And this heightened efficiency is often without a defined purpose: It is urgency absent direction, strategy, or goal. We strive, but never arrive.

The Efficiency Effect:* A perpetual postponement of essential benefits, including but not limited to interpersonal connection—stemming from a valuation of *Momentum* over *the Moment.

Try selling this one. If the rest of your life were a paying job, it would be as if you punched in early, worked evenings and weekends, skipped vacations, and sneezed your way through—*in sickness and in health, right?*—waving off any compensation with an, "Oh, that's OK. You can pay me later."

If we were describing your passion, e.g., "This doesn't *feel* like work"—beautiful! But when the wide-angle shot is of you racing on a hamster wheel, hoping that a finish line complete with palm trees, an umbrella drink, and your family and closest friends will come into view—it doesn't look like such a smart choice, does it? Postponing enjoyment, fulfillment, and connection—our essential human goals—for indefinite periods of time, will eventually deplete our resources and reserves, leaving one sad, hungry little hamster.

Identifying Negative Efficiencies

Let's examine how over-efficiency manifests and how this Efficiency Effect, can isolate us. Where and how you spend your time and energy is payment toward whatever it is you hope to achieve—with your overall life path as your biggest purchase. *It certainly has the longest payment plan.* If the sum total of all our effort seems less than it should be, perhaps we aren't investing wisely. *This is one case where a **high** interest rate is preferred.* Oftentimes, our pattern of daily choices inadvertently depletes our reserves and disconnects us from replenishing resources.

Which of these negative efficiencies do you recognize in your life?

1) Acquaintances Over Friendships

Whether the news is good or bad, we want to share it. It seems instinctive to verbally replay momentous events with another human being.

If a tree falls in the forest and nobody tweeted, did it really happen?

But for a disconnected person, it can feel like a stumbling grab for the stair rail that isn't there.

Our utilitarian approach gives us many casual acquaintances, but virtual proximity is no measure of emotional investment and true attachment. Many of us look well-connected on Facebook but have few listening friends.

Sometimes out of desperate need, the lonely will try to tap into online sympathy and mine those virtual reservoirs of contacts with a "TMI" online post or two—"*Why can't a smart, fairly attractive mature woman find a decent, faithful guy?*" or "*Be strong and know that (blah, blah, blah...plagiarized quote of the week),*" but such monologues of misery are discomfiting and, ultimately, perpetuate the disconnection. These heart-baring seekers need real listening friends, and contrary to popular instinct, there is *not* an app for that. You can't pull slow-cooked ribs from a microwave oven.

All of us have need for human-to-human contact on the things that matter, and sometimes, even on the things that don't. It isn't always about the content. More often the value is grounded in the connective aspect of conversation.

With our cell phones, laptops, and social media accounts, it *seems* like there should be an endless supply of ears just waiting to listen. But unless you work to develop some texture in the relationships and build depth with a few chosen contacts, there are often few to none. A recent study published in the *American Sociological Review* reported one in four of its respondents described themselves as living without access to a confidante. And when immediate family members were excluded, *less than half* had someone with whom to share their most important personal information![19]

Unfortunately, those personalized subject lines in your email inbox are more likely to be filter-hopping scam spam than actual personal communiqués. Have some big news? Who are you going to call? Oh sure, you could reach out to the coworker you lunch with, but be honest—it would be a bit of a stretch without plastic forks in hand.

Guess it can wait till Monday. No, Thursday. Forgot she's using personal days next week.

And that Mom you "*Hey batter, batter!*"-ed with through baseball season... maybe you even began saving one another adjacent seats in the bleachers, but your boys attend different schools, and it's unlikely you'll bump into one another anywhere at this point. You might have knocked around the idea of getting together after that last playoff game, but it got busy, and now two months have gone by. *I wonder if she's still dealing with that crazy neighbor and could use some sanity-saving commiseration?*

It would be kind of weird to just call out of the blue without any games on the calendar.

Our busy lives frequently relegate potential friends to the default "acquaintance" status. *Subtitle: missed opportunity.*

We have a lot of these.

Our teams lack depth. If family ties are weak, broken, or non-existent, many of us have no bench. Fumble a big client call? Having trouble with a romance? Who will care? *Besides your boss in the first case...and, also, in the second if there's any overlap.*

It becomes a reach toward who will tolerate you and your concerns instead of who can talk, listen, and share a burden with you.

Several years ago, I stood in my master bedroom, tears streaming as I scrolled through local phone contacts, thinking, "*There has to be somebody I can talk to.*" But there wasn't. An out-of-state aunt and cousin were wonderful about providing long-distance support at my lowest points, but those phone calls highlighted to me that my life had a huge cavernous space that could never be filled by one person alone.

I had allowed myself to grow disconnected on a large scale. I was happier to slip in and out of school meetings and my home rather than risk an awkward revelation of my life's messy moments. And there were a *lot* of messy moments: the three-year divorce process, a heartbreaking affair, deaths of loved ones, a mini-series' worth of extended family drama. My life looked nothing like I'd expected or wanted it to be. Answering the simplest "How are you?" felt complicated. Sifting and sorting through what to share with whom required more energy than I had access to. It was far easier to head for the exit with a quick wave—or worse, to slip out unnoticed.

Isolation was self-perpetuating, and over time, I bumped into obvious points at which connection was needed and missed. Here are the three *Friends Needed* moments that troubled me most.

In Case of Emergency. For me, "I.C.E" stood for "I Can't Even E-magine." It was embarrassing! And very sad. An emergency worker checking my contacts for frequently-called numbers was more likely to discover palatable Chinese carryout than the number of a worried friend.

And I dreaded the "Contact Information" portion of medical forms! Those fill-in-the-blank lines provoked anxiety. *Three? Do they really need three entire people?* The request for my personal backup system felt intrusive—a jab at my disconnection. The form said "Contacts," but the underlying question was: "Who are your friends?"

Furtively I'd scroll through my phone, searching my most recent conversations for a name and a number, sometimes resorting to purposeful illegibility, scrawling the names and scrambling the numbers. And then, my pen would hover over "relationship to patient." *Acquaintance? "Friend"* felt presumptuous. *At minimum you should be able to answer "dog person" or "cat person," and you can't even state with certainty how many kids she has!* And even had I been confident in using these individuals' contact info, I wavered on their true availability should I experience palpitations exceptional enough to require hospitalization. I imagined one of my listed acquaintance "friends" hemming and hawing, *"That's awful. You said 'Heather,' right? Reddish-brown hair? Um, does she have any family listed? No? Well, I just ordered the pizza but can try and swing by after dinner, I guess."*

In Case of Happiness. And on the other end of that rainbow...there sits your pot of joy. *Nice!* Yep, occasionally something beautiful drops in, igniting glorious sparks of hope and delight. And it's *hard* to confine those effervescent victory moments! They should be shared like bubbling champagne! But it's almost easier to share a challenge or tragedy, depending on its degree of difficulty on the misery scale. Bona fide trials will at least garner sympathy—*but are not to be confused with "Can you believe it! I lost another pound, dammit. It's so hard having a naturally high metabolism!"*

Sharing a happy moment—a success, win, or blessing—will likely be construed as so much braggadocio. And it kind of is. Absent a mutual relationship in which you're each actively supporting one another, how could you expect a mere acquaintance to muster real appreciation for your happiness? Not that some won't genuinely enjoy another's unrelated success—but to *expect* that from someone who doesn't know you well, and more importantly, someone whom you don't know that well yourself? It's presumptuous and potentially further isolating. The indiscriminate celebrant is like a firecracker set off in a residential neighborhood, sparking confusion—"*Where did that come from?*" and concern—"*Let's get inside, kids.*"

Help Needed. Rides to the airport? Car trouble? That kind of "Can you help me out?" phone call was out of my league.

"You don't have a friend with a pickup truck? There's kind of a steep delivery charge, ma'am."

It was always easier to call a cab, wait out the repair, get a rental, or just grimace and pay.

Non-emergency emotional needs were the worst: when Grandma was dying, when I was gripped by divorce decisions and dealing with an unethical lawyer, and as I took first steps into developing my writing career. Without sounding boards through which to channel and diffuse the steady stream of emotion and information, fears surged and occasionally paralyzed me.

I had a few contacts but yearned for a casual but sincere "How are you doing?" from someone who really wanted to know the answer.

2) Use of Old Filters

Loneliness is awkward. Nothing fits. It's less about being alone and more about having no context for connection within your environment. When we're overly efficient, we've less time to establish any sort of framework and tend to run new scenarios through old familiar filters, further solidifying those "I'm an outsider" feelings.

I remember walking into a school meeting shortly after my divorce, certain that all eyes would home in on the naked ring finger on my left hand. My discomfort had to be obvious as I apologetically scanned for empty seats with a tentative, eager-to-please smile, cautious of intruding on anyone's space with any actual eye contact. As the mother of a student, I certainly belonged there, but my demeanor suggested I'd crashed the meeting. *Because who wouldn't long to spend ninety uncomfortable minutes on a small plastic chair during the dinner hour on a Wednesday?*

It's hard to be around women like that. They need more encouragement than can be shared with a simple smile, and they take non-response as negative feedback. Their discomfort makes others uncomfortable and becomes the fuel for that self-perpetuating spiral downwards.

But many times, the "outsider" feeling has less to do with present circumstances than it does with old programming. If childhood memories of exclusion or inattentive or unappreciative parents dwell just beneath the surface, it's likely that the first surge of discomfort will exert a little pressure on that old feeling, releasing it anew; the old feeling is repackaged but with much of its original freshness.

For me, that school meeting triggered time travel back to middle school number two. Once again, I was wandering the cafeteria with a lunch tray, wishing I could just disappear and wake up when my face had cleared up and my glacially growing breasts had gotten a fair chance to catch up with my nose. In the years since that unmemorable eighth grade debut, I'd traded Clearasil for moisturizer and discovered underwire bras. But inside? I was still the new kid, hoping to be noticed with the quiet welcome due any awkward but kind wallflower.

But a *lot* of us have felt—or feel—that way.

Unvarnished Disclosure: Always the Runner-Up

While a firstborn, Barb always felt like the afterthought.

"I was never quite good enough. I was never one of the pretty girls. When I think about the popular girls...I was never one of those."

Overachiever Barb had never measured up. "I was my grandma's favorite. And my mom—we had a great relationship."

But her dad was difficult.

"We never really bonded well. Which is weird, because I tried so darn hard! I tried everything! I guess I'm stubborn. I kept thinking if I just do more. Do better. He'll notice. But he never did."

Quiet and studious, Barb graduated second in her high school class.

"I wasn't first."

She had hoped things would change when she went away to college but even with a fresh start she still felt as if she were just beyond what really mattered—"on the fringe," as she had described her high school experience with the "popular kids" group, whom she discovered, years later, had excluded her from numerous parties.

"They were afraid I'd tell on them. I can't believe I was such a goody two shoes. I might not have gone, but I wouldn't have told on them!"

As was her bent, Barb blamed herself for the unkindness of others.

She remembered her dad coming to watch one of her tennis matches on a campus court. He was less than supportive. "You know how in tennis you're supposed to win the point? Well, my dad's comment was, 'You can't be that good if you can't keep the ball going.'"

"I was *winning!*"

We laughed, but it wasn't that funny.

In all the years that followed, Barb kept trying to fit in. To be part of a group.

"When did I first feel that way?" she repeated. "I don't remember ever *not* feeling like that. I was always on the fringe. Close enough to tag along but never really one of the 'cool kids.' But a few years ago, it finally happened."

Barb had hung out with the "popular" guys at a business conference. "I remember driving home and going, 'Wow!' I was thrilled that I'd been able to hang out with the 'cool kids.' It's kind of pathetic that it made such a huge impression on me, but it's because I'd never felt that before."

She paused to sip her wine. "I still don't feel like I'm quite good enough. But I'm getting closer."

Barb had an odd conversation with a cousin soon after her father died about ten years ago. "I'd called to tell her that Dad was gone, and Sue went on and on about how I was my dad's favorite, that he had adored me and always wanted the best for me. He didn't want my sisters to feel slighted." Barb was at a loss. The disconnect between her dad's words and her own reality was clear.

He overcompensated?

She shrugged. Was silent for a moment as she thought it over. "I guess. But *I* was the one who ended up feeling slighted. And it has impacted all of my relationships with men. I guess I've kind of been stuck in that."

As a Cabernet Coach, Barb was the first to make our Wednesday night gatherings a recurring calendar entry. We discovered and developed our bond over a high-top table and glasses of cabernet at her favorite restaurant bar. Her ready embrace of the Cabernet Coach concept confirmed my suspicion that I wasn't the only one in need of stronger more consistent connection.

Her personal evolution over the past few years has been remarkable.

As Barb grew relationships in her service groups and amongst her Cabernet Coaches, these friends reflected back a truer image of "Barb" than she was seeing in her bathroom mirror or hearing in that endless replay of her dad's criticisms. Her essential qualities—humor, intellect, and kindness—manifested in a quiet but sounder confidence. Her whole demeanor relaxed, and her real beauty grew more obvious. She updated her hairstyle and dress, laughed more, and began to expect more. Recognizing the dead-end nature of her law firm career path, Barb came up with an exit plan and eventually transitioned to having her own practice. She even began distancing herself from a problematic long-term love relationship that had left her unavailable to new beginnings.

Recently, she assessed her journey as we sat in my family room. "I'm not all the way there yet. But I'm making progress."

3) Distracted Lifestyle

A wandering eye can be a relationship killer. At the very least, that drifting gaze will put a damper on dinner, but these days, the interloping distraction is often sitting right next to the dinner napkin. *"Excuse me...got a text."* It's vibrating and flashing a steady stream of other options. *"Sorry, I really need to take this."* The texting dinner date couple is a sad cliché of disconnection.

A Baylor University survey on phone snubbing or "phubbing" revealed the distracted behavior to be a significant source of relationship dissatisfaction.[20] Nearly half of the respondents considered a partner's smartphone to be significant competition, vying for attention mid-conversation and even in the bedroom—candlelight replaced by the flickering of a cell phone screen, perhaps.

It isn't you. It isn't even me. It's my iPhone.

The quick glance toward phone or laptop is easily justified: *"This will only take a minute." "I'm just monitoring my work emails." "I only scroll the headlines when we aren't talking."*

Temporary suspension of a face-to-face interaction for electronic communication is accepted enough that people reflexively pause mid-sentence when they hear the buzz of a cell phone. Our children *hate* the confusing mixed message—*You're important to me, but I choose to share my attention with (fill in the blank).* Sibling rivalry? These days it's more like a competition with the whole planet!

We officially banned cell phones at our dinner table after annoying one another to no end with discourteous behavior. *Except to challenge the occasional "not ready for Webster" word during one of our cutthroat Scrabble games.*

If our tag-along cell phones were little humans, blatantly interrupting and dancing across table-tops demanding to be heard, we'd raise an eyebrow and glance around for the negligent parent permitting such rude behavior. But because they're electronic, we have indulged them like spoiled children.

What we once negatively characterized as an interruption has been reframed as "instant availability"—but at significant cost. We *surf* headlines and *skim* articles. We may *prioritize* "limited engagements," but the imposed limit is not as much the external timeframe, but rather, our own wandering attention.

It *seems* efficient to maintain awareness of more than the present moment, as if we're getting a head start on whatever comes next, but this state of continual anticipation and preparedness creates drag as our brains struggle to keep up. *Wait a minute. Who's Mark? I thought you said we were talking to Sarah?*

A joint study on cognitive distraction generated by use of in-vehicle navigation systems by the American Automobile Association and the University of Utah found that a driver's focus could be compromised by lingering impairment for as long as 27 seconds after using voice commands to select music and phone numbers.[21] Reading a headline or generating a text response requires *far* more brain power than *"Dial Home,"* but we're flying between verbal and texted conversations like we've got wings and a wand. Only, of course we don't. Our brains must reengage via our original equipment. We're smart, capable, and committed, but it gets progressively harder to keep up with the flow of traffic—society's frenetic life pace—when we keep switching our own direction.

Absent clear goals for our heightened dependency on cell phones, internet, and social media, and with the explosion of information on demand and "instant everything," our small sacrifices of time and attention inevitably weaken, diminish, and derail real life experiences. We've traded the panoramic view for the smaller screen of a smartphone, and the subsequent digital amnesia obstructs our ability to encode present moments into long-term memories.[22] Ironically, we readily forget that which we seek to establish as memorable.

An unrelenting multi-tasking approach will damage relationships, short-circuit our basic focusing skills, and diminish our appreciation of the present. And these "small sacrifices"—of attention, time, and engagement—can easily grow into a life-crushing relinquishment of connection.

Our grudging acceptance of continuous distraction sends a clear and disconnecting message to others and to our own selves.

4) Pleasure Postponement

The Efficiency Effect has also put an anaconda-like squeeze on our joy. We set up impossible parameters for ourselves:

"I'll join book club when life settles down a little more."

"I'll get back into a gym routine again once I'm caught up at work."

"I'll catch up with (*fill in the blank*) on my next quiet afternoon."

Or we never bother to fully define the goals:

"I need to get more organized."

"I have to get all my errands done."

"I need to do something fun."

The sacrifices continue, but the reward never comes. We dangle the chosen carrot just beyond our reach—pushing off the jackpot of enjoyment to the other end of a rainbow that arches up higher and higher—leaving us in a continual climb.

As a five-year old, my daughter Hannah picked out "Dorothy" shoes[23]—glittering red Mary Janes. She immediately declared them her "favorites" and skipped from checkout to car, clutching the bag close on her lap all the way home before parking them front and center on her closet floor. I couldn't wait to see her spin out a pleated skirt on the toes of her new treasures.

But she chose an older pair of sandals for church the following Sunday.

"You aren't going to wear your new shoes?"

"They'll get dirty. We're going out on the playground today."

And then a couple of days later.

"Your new red shoes would match that dress perfectly!"

"Um, I think it's going to rain. They'll get wet."

And so it went for another month.

I finally asked her if she was ever going to wear them.

"Did you decide you don't like them after all?"

"I love them. They're the prettiest shoes I've ever had!"

"Then, why haven't you worn them?"

"I can't. They have sparkles. I don't want to ruin them. They won't be new anymore."

For some reason, Hannah couldn't allow herself to experience her new shoes. Eventually, we returned them and found some she could actually wear. It made both of us sad at the time, but years later, we laughed and pondered the underlying lesson about indefinitely postponing our pleasure.

This, sadly, is common "grownup" behavior. An overly-efficient lifestyle leads many of us to never enjoy our declared "favorites."

In my talks, I refer to this as "Someday Living." Many adult singles postpone their biggest life goals and dreams with the hope that someone else, the guy or gal of their dreams, will take them there. We also hold basic pleasures at arm's length in deference to a work/reward system that got stuck on work, work, work. Whether there's an "I don't deserve it" or "I'll enjoy it more later" underneath it all, the "toil without treasure" mode is detrimental to our overall emotional balance.

Unvarnished Disclosure: I Can't Even Celebrate

We met by the breakfast buffet, recognized each other from previous networking events and a mutual friendship, and navigated past the bagels, biscuits, and questionable bowl of vanilla yogurt toward the fruit platter at table's end.

"So, remind me what you do?" I asked, spooning strawberry bits onto a tiny paper plate.

"I'm in logistics. Basically, I deal with UPS, trucking companies, manufacturers...and get things to other places. I coordinate shipments, schedules, transportation—that kind of thing."

"What company are you with?"

"Well, I'm actually doing it myself. One company employs me, but I'm working toward being completely on my own." Mindy smiled. "I can't wait."

"That's great! And pretty impressive," I commented. "What's your timeline?"

Mindy gestured toward one of the tablecloth-clad high-top tables arranged throughout the room. "Want to set ourselves up over there?"

It seemed like a good idea. Holding coffee, a food plate, and my balance while in heels always feels a little daring to me.

"So, tell me more."

"Well, my goal is the end of the year, but it's September 18th and . . ." She paused and shook her head. "No. It will be the end of this year," she corrected herself. Her shoulders slumped. "I hate it when I do that!"

"I imagine there are a lot of things to get in place."

"Yes, but a lot of great things *did* fall into place last week. But, it's like I can't allow myself to enjoy it! I really hate that about myself. It's going well, but I'm always focused on what hasn't happened instead of appreciating what I've managed to accomplish."

"I get that. You can be so focused on the goal, you forget to toggle the off switch from time to time."

"Yeah! I need to remember to breathe every now and then! On my bathroom mirror, I have a saying, 'Pause. Breathe deeply—'" Head shake. "I can't remember the third one."

I waited a moment. She shook her head again and gave it up.

"Sometimes I have to schedule a little slow breathing for myself," I admitted. "I just type in these stress-free zones and try my best to honor them—I finally came up with some visualizations that really work for me."

"It's really bad that I'm not appreciating what I've worked so hard for."

I nodded. "It's hard. When you have a goal, it's so easy to postpone the "pause and appreciate." Something always needs to be done. Sometimes it's just a load of laundry, but we often prioritize the wrong things."

"I just want to do it all, but I need to be grateful."

Mindy's words resonated; I was sure to congratulate her on her success before I left.

Later that day, I Googled "Pause, Breathe . . ." The missing word was "Relax."

I mentally added, "Appreciate."

With a default future focus, we give up the moment we are in for a hypothetical "to be continued . . ." moment that never comes, living in a state of constant preparation and infrequent participation.

Not surprisingly, this has impacted our energy and ability to connect. Exhaustion has become our "normal," because there is no finish line. Enjoyment of friendships is relegated to the afterparty that never arrives.

5) Pressure on the Primary

Five of the top ten stressors ranked in The Holmes-Raye Stress Inventory Social Readjustment Rating Scale are marriage-related, with the death of a spouse at the top and divorce and marital separation tagging along in second and third place. Getting married is the seventh most stressful life event you're likely to experience, and reconciling with that guy who forgot the anniversary date of stressor number seven rates ninth.[24] But you knew this...maybe not the statistics, but clearly, a long-term love relationship is guaranteed hard work with no assurance of the outcome. It's a huge investment, and we often want strong emotional assurances that what impacts us matters—*really matters*—to our chosen someone.

Without a few sandbags on that balloon, expectations can quickly rise out of control.

Even the most loving romantic partner will fail on the listening end—or simply exceed his or her bandwidth after a half dozen convolutions of the same story. *C'mon, I'm not the only one who repeats herself!*

Ideally, married women and those in long-term committed relationships find listening ears in their partner *and* in additional supportive friendships—because strapping *all* of your connection and sharing expectations onto one person will dull even the best-intentioned mate's receptivity. Quite frankly, *all* of *your stuff* is too much for one person to handle alone. You're familiar with the "Don't put all your eggs in one basket" adage? Similarly, don't pour all your hopes and dreams, happiness, and stories into a single relationship either.

With less time available to invest in outside friendships, however, some couples gradually retreat into a cozy bubble-for-two, limiting their social activity almost exclusively to that primary relationship. While sustaining a healthy relationship through the inherent ups and downs of life is laudable, dialing down your interactions—your overall connectivity—to one individual is risky for at least a couple of reasons.

First, while an isolated "just the two of us" biosphere might seem the romantic ideal at the euphoric start of a romantic relationship, relying on recycled table talk tuned into the 24/7 "Us" channel will eventually deplete the oxygen in that little bubble. Lip-on-lip kissing beats a peck on the cheek, to be sure, but mouth-to-mouth breathing is considered an emergency resuscitation measure. Don't rely on one single person to sustain your life and levels of joy. Temporarily? Say he has a job crisis and needs a little TLC outside the public spotlight of explanatory conversation, or you're wrestling with a disappointment and need some privacy as you regroup. A short-term retreat-and-regroup is understandable and will hopefully deepen that bond that drew you together in the first place. Just keep in mind that limiting your inhale *exclusively* to one other person's exhale will soon suck all the good air out of Utopia.

Unvarnished Disclosure: Panic and Pressure

Andrea called as I was ending a lengthy run through South Mountain Park near Scottsdale, Arizona. I had time to retrieve my water bottle, gulp it down, and amble down to the hotel pool before a response was required—or even possible.

"It's over!" she cried. "He's leaving me. I can't handle this anymore. What will I do? How can he just quit? I know I have a hard time with stress. He knows I can't deal with so much at once. It's just the way I am, and S-S-Sam has put us through so much!

"All I did was ask him why he hadn't planned anything special for this weekend, when he knows it's so important to me and he-he-he *knows* I need a break! He said he was tired and that I should just call a friend, but he *knows* I don't have t-time for friends! And he said he didn't feel like doing *anything!* I said, 'all weekend?!' And he said he just wanted some time by him*self!* By himself! Without me!

"I said, 'That's pretty selfish,' 'cause it IS! He has no idea how hard this is for me! He just shook his head at me, and I-I know I shouldn't have pushed it, but I j-just couldn't help it! I said, 'You think *I'm* the selfish one?! After everything I do for this family and when work is *so* crazy and I have that MRI check next week...you think I'm selfish for wanting to relax with you and take a break from all of that? You aren't even *worried* about me!'"

Now seated on the pool deck, I removed my socks and shoes and began swirling my toes in the water as I waited her out.

"I told him I need just a little more of his attention. Two hours later, he said he can't do it anymore. That I went too far again, and that he just wants to be alone!" She sobbed into the phone. "I know I have to do better controlling my t-temper, but there's just too much stress. It isn't fair, and he knew I was emotional when he married me! Now he says he's quitting!"

"He said he doesn't want to be married?" I navigated my wording with care, avoiding the "D" word.

"He said he didn't know! I asked him if he loved me, and he said his love is kind of 'buried' right now which is the same thing! We've been married ten years, and suddenly he doesn't know if he wants to be married to me? How am I supposed to live with that? And you're out of town, and I can't tell anyone else! I'm going out of my mind!"

"Do you want to make this better?"

"Of course, I do! But I can't. He doesn't love me anymore." *Uncontrollable sobbing.*

I hurt *for* her, but like her husband Scott, I felt some collateral pain as well. Andrea tended to be a crisis-caller. Scott was her best friend—only friend, really—and while she occasionally considered him also to be her worst enemy, she was often the villain in her own drama because she insisted he appear in every scene.

Like many of us, she had scrambled over big obstacles her whole life. But to Andrea, each obstruction felt deliberately placed, an affront to her deserved happiness. In perpetual catch-up mode to retrieve what had been "taken," Andrea's focus had been on accumulating all of her "good life" elements. Husband Scott was one, son Sam another.

Andrea simply didn't have time for friends or any sort of life apart from her family and work. Everything bounced off of the same wall, and this over-efficiency was making a sizeable dent in her marriage relationship. I feared for her marriage and wondered what she would do without it.

Second, not to be unduly morbid, but even "till death do us part" has a natural and unknown ending point, does it not? An eventual, jointly-timed departure from this world is unlikely. Most commonly, half of a couple will eventually face the challenge of living as a widow or widower.

Apart from newborn babies, Valentine's Day rhymes, and future scientific breakthroughs, no one can be anybody's *everything.* If we channel all of our heart-to-heart material toward a single person—a spouse, lover, or even a best friend—it's more tsunami than conversational flow. When we lack other people in our lives, there can be an unhealthy tendency toward overuse of the connections we do have. We can develop quite the sideways lean.

6) Space-Filler Choices

It seems counterintuitive. Busy people seem so well-connected! But have you ever noticed, they're never connected to *you?* The predominant direction is usually "away." They "touch base" with you before invariably launching on to the next appointment, obligation, or responsibility.

It may present as an infilling, but the expected fullness never really materializes. Just more busyness. The net result is more space in the space.

I've done it. How about you?

In my self-designated roles of Super Mom, Wife, and Mega-Volunteer, space scared me. In a house cluttered with Matchbox cars and glitter glue—traded later for soccer cleats and track spikes—an overabundance of physical space was never an issue. Emotional space, however, was hard to avoid.

I could deal with vomit and school project deadlines—"*You need to have a completed paper maché replica of the Ohio Cavern for third period* ***tomorrow****?!*"

It was harder to handle what was crowding the space in my head.

Our marriage was shaky, although neither my ex-husband or I would have said so. The tremors were easily attributed to a busy stage of life and dealing with some prolonged conflict in my extended family. Normal stuff. But then came the back-to-back deaths of my parents and my grandfather's stage 4 brain cancer diagnosis—grief upon grief and more family drama.

In the past, emotional dysfunctions served as our wobbly gravitational force, adhering us together with mutual need. But this time, self-preservation generated a much stronger centrifugal energy and began to pull us apart.

Wading through a rising tide of loss, I poured myself into helping my grandparents in Florida and then into regaining the time lost from my kids with every bit I had left. One-way flights, uncertainty, growing guilt that I couldn't be everywhere at once...My ex-husband, unable to find a reset button with which to fix it all, began seeking refuge at work. Isolated by my grief—*so lonely* now amidst this flurry of caring for others, I spun between feeling desperately needy and stoically independent. I'd no sense of which side would prevail, but "needy" felt a closer match to my inner confusion. Even though I sensed my need was for a connectedness unavailable in our marriage.

The space grew like a nervous perspiration stain. It looked bad. Smelled bad. I didn't know what to do with it.

So, after Grandpa died, I took on more. Lots of volunteering for the kids' schools and our church. I gardened and ran like a maniac. We traveled. I obsessed over anything I could conjure up that would deflect from the deepening issues in our marriage, carefully avoiding thought triggers such as romantic movies and books, and the happiness of other married couples we knew. I filled the space in my head—with music when I ran and with spy thriller fiction during the rare quiet moments.

If there's no time to think, there's no problem, right?

But there was this blank expanse on my bedroom wall that I'd stare down when I was feeling brave. I'd look at that patch of creamy bareness and wonder how I'd fill my life if I had any choice in the way I lived it. I confined a lot of "what if"s to that spot, like an Etch-a-Sketch that I'd scribble on in moments of silent misery and then carefully shake away before anyone else saw the pictures. My busyness was essential to maintaining the status quo. And those brief moments of Etch-a-Sketch reflection were dangerous—revealing to me, all the more, how much space I had to fill.

Sometimes Superwoman gets busy saving the world so that she won't have to figure out how to save herself. Many of us do this: We avoid difficult decisions and painful reflection by making "Space-Filler" choices.

***Space-Filler Choices:* Options we value not for their effectiveness, but instead for their proximity and volume—allowing us to postpone hard choices and inadvertently prolong our emotional turmoil.**

Disconnection in marriage? People have babies and affairs. They obsess about extraneous details and buy things they don't need as they shop for bigger and bigger houses. They work harder and focus on—or even generate—outside stresses to deflect attention from what they aren't ready to face.

Outside of marriage? After a divorce, perhaps? The newly single adult often obsesses over the sins of the departing partner or speed-dates toward his/her replacement. Thoughtful reflection is rarely part of the initial response. It hurts. We seek sedatives and painkillers.

Filling the brain with other matter—TV watching, loud music, reading, fitness routines, other people's problems, health issues, work—all of these allow us to tell the elephant in the room, "Just a minute." Indefinitely.

Unvarnished Disclosure: No Time for Friends

Carol worked. She credits twenty-five wedding anniversaries to her typical seventy-hour work week.

The marriage never had a chance. "He didn't love me. We had a ten-year age difference. He targeted me, a younger woman, because he wanted children. We had sex only to get me pregnant, and he was indifferent after he had 'his' children. I think we had sex less than 15 times in our 25-year marriage. Eventually, he told me that I was unattractive, unlovable, that 'no one knows you like I do,' and that he didn't even *like* me."

As a devout Christian, divorce didn't seem like an option. "It was 'God hates divorce,' so buck up, move on. I had no choice."

And no friends—Carol suffered alone. Her one close friend, Abby, lived miles away in Nevada. "It was pride. Embarrassment," Carol said of her initial non-disclosure. Abby wouldn't have judged her, but Carol judged herself.

"I finally tried counseling four years in and was told to submit, quit working, and lots of other foolishness. After getting that kind of response three or four times, I just withdrew. 'If that's your answer, I'm not going to divulge my problem.'"

But it was lonely. "In those twenty-five years, I didn't have a single local woman I could call or text and say, 'let's go to a movie' or 'want to have dinner?' Oh sure, there were moms I sat next to on the bleachers during the kids' games; there were work colleagues, but I couldn't share the details of my life. So, I worked harder. I couldn't say I needed friends if I didn't have time for them."

She withdrew and narrowed her focus. "I had three beautiful kids. I decided to just throw myself into raising them."

And her work. "My ex-husband quit working six years into our marriage. In theory, he was going to help me with my business, but in reality, his world was TV and our kids. He never worked again. In essence, I became an income and domestic servant."

One hundred twenty additional pounds later, Carol was filled with disgust and shame. "If my own husband found me repulsive—who would/could love me? So I worked."

"It filled my time. But not my heart."

Carol has now learned the value of transparency. "Only in the past few years have I learned to be vulnerable. I've been divorced two years now. I feel like I've moved at warp speed because I was very intentional in pursuing healing."

"One of the big early hurdles I crossed, the hardest thing to admit, was my vulnerability. My woundedness. To finally say, 'Yes, I need friends. I can't do this alone."

"I can't be Superwoman and pretend this doesn't hurt. It was life-changing to admit that friendships are essential to my emotional health."

7) Touch-and-Go Connections

When we're at our efficient best, gathering all our options for "someday," our real-time physical interactions tend to be more "Tag—you're 'It'" than genuine engagement. Even our face-to-face interactions can tend to resemble the "clickable connections" of our online lives. Scrambling to bail out the inflow of tasks on our To-Do lists, we dart into groups and gatherings, intent on making the minimum requirement—*Where's the signup sheet?*—focused on affirming that our attendance is duly noted as our brains get a head start on solving tomorrow's problems. I admit it. Periodically, I've valued hitting "send" or leaving a voicemail as a responsibility handoff more than as an outreach toward real communication. Blame it on multi-tasking, but this is less of a mind*set* than symptomatic of an *unsettled* mind, distracted from the present moment by a prospective one.

And no one's fooling anybody! We all have an instinct for when we're being check-listed off somebody else's agenda. That "lips only" smile and sideways glance sends a less than cordial message. Now, the true meaning may be that somebody is overloaded or simply having an off day, but the Touch-and-Go interaction says, "I have bigger priorities."

Established friendships may bear a short period of Touch-and-Go with little long-term consequence. But even with "we never miss a beat" friends, there's a gap to restore. And our more efficient interactions, leaving no time for side trips into a genuine "How are you" and "*Who* are you," lessen the likelihood of developing new bonds. The birth of a friendship is often serendipitous—a random click between *attentive* kindred spirits. Much like romantic attachments, we can't predict when a connection might happen, but minimizing our interactions to butterfly-like bursts of intensity will certainly prevent them.

It's like giving the world a mobile version of our self that isn't web-ready—a *lite* version that's short on engaging social features. We're less memorable—and if remembered, it might be for a less-than-exemplary social shortcut. Ever had a "Who was *that*?!" reaction to your own "S'cuse me—I'm in a hurry!" behavior? Not a good feeling!

And moving at warp speed makes it kind of hard to remember the names and faces, doesn't it? Admittedly, some of our brain lag can be tied to overfilling the container. *For instance, why can't I just dump the childhood phone number and reallocate that segment of grey matter to remembering parking spaces?* However, a good deal of our hemming and hawing at a *second* meeting—*"Uh-oh, you'll need to introduce yourself. She works with Dan, but I can't remember her name"*—lies with our inattention at the beginning.

No one remembers us, and we remember no one unless we see an immediate need for them.

Ouch.

8) Immobilization

Do you remember the Gravitron? *Hint: nausea-inducing if paired with corndogs and a milkshake.* No doubt there's now a bigger, badder version than the amusement park ride I remember, but as an astronaut wannabe (ultimately deterred by the lack of hiking trails off my current planet and a dread of college physics), the science alone fascinated me. *And when it comes to pushing the bounds of Earth's gravitational pull, I give extra points for accessibility and convenience.* The Gravitron was always a "must ride." Its positive G-force was a closer cousin to a rocket lift-off than the negative G-force of a stomach-flipping roller coaster.

Basically, Gravitron-ers walked, or were dragged, into a brightly painted cylinder. If there was a waiting line—no worries, as the inner sanctum could hold 75 or more sweating, squealing riders. When the ride operator deigned to open the gate, we filed in and strapped ourselves somewhere along the single circular wall—*hopefully, across from a cute boy we could then pretend not to notice for the next 90 seconds or so.* Eventually, after the kid on the mic ran through his spiel of "thou shalt not"s, the room began to rotate, accelerating and flattening us to the wall as, inevitably, the rider with the highest, shrillest voice began shrieking hysterically.

With the whole room spinning right along with us, there wasn't a sense of dizziness so much as the feeling that our ears were the only things keeping our faces from doing a 180-degree slide around our heads—*and if you dislike the way a high-powered hand dryer reveals loose skin, a Gravitron ride is inadvisable.* In moments, hands and feet were plastered to the wall, and toe wiggling was out of the question. *Testing, testing...OK, I get it. I'm a bug on a windshield.*

Our lives can gain that Gravitron-like feel—as we're immobilized by obligations, responsibilities, all the "should"s that fly our way, and plain old interruptions. Opportunity Clutter, the Efficiency Effect, that narrowing funnel of time...They work in tandem to spin our world out of control, pin us in place, and isolate us—separating us from others like a lab sample in a centrifuge. We can't move because we're needed in all directions. Everything feels completely out of our control. We're captives to some disinterested, texting ride operator who's just killing time until his lunch break as we wait, helpless and exposed, for someone else to find the emergency stop switch.

Whether we're actually alone or not doesn't really matter. Our growing lack of connection makes us *feel* alone—lonely. We're alone in a crowd, no matter how many people are in the room.

Connection Point

Efficiency seems practical. Noble, even. During the lengthy 2015-16 presidential debates, I often combined my current affairs intake with a little exercise—by adding to my step count or using free weights while listening (in disbelief) with my utterly flabbergasted first-time voter son, Matt. How practical of me, right?

But scanning emails while watching the NBA playoffs with Matt? Not so good. He grew justifiably annoyed at my ill-timed questions—*What's the score? Who's that guy again?* Because it demonstrated, rather clearly, that I'm a marginal and occasionally inconsiderate sports fan. *Unless I'm an active participant or once diapered any of the players.*

Where does the Efficiency Effect show up in your life? Are your conversations often repetitive—a recycling of the same pat pleasantries that get you through an exchange and on with your day? Does one friend or family member function as your sole emotional repository? Do you spend fifty weeks of the year counting down to your two weeks of vacation? Do you often sense that you're halfway in on far more than you can manage, under-equipped and overwhelmed, as you survey your teetering tower of "should"s?

Believe it or not, the world *will go on* if you politely resign from a committee or opt out of holiday cookie baking. Much better that you approach life rested, fully engaged, and able to offer the best version of You.

Or maybe you gravitate toward space-fillers to avoid something—opting for perfection or uber-productivity over connecting those floating, unformed thoughts or feelings in your peripheral vision. Perfectly understandable. Gathering it all into daylight could get messy, and then you'd have to spend some time sorting it out, right? And who knows what could jump out of those shadows. Is your heart ready for this? Maybe you fear, as I did, that something could change, either within you or in the way you perceive the world around you. Busyness may seem less disruptive. More manageable. But the truth is, it takes a tremendous amount of energy to ignore those emotional "elephants." And keep in mind that the muffled head noise is actually your heart attempting to communicate with your brain regarding something it finds unacceptable. Snub your heart at your own risk. In my case, that communication shutdown led to depression, anxiety, and wasted opportunity.

What might your Etch-a-Sketch picture look like if you were to fill it in with your private thoughts? Take a good hard look at it before you shake it away. Make sure your heart and brain have open communication.

What joys have you postponed? *Someday, I'm going to pull out those paint brushes, look up that friend from college, snorkel in the Caribbean...* Allow me to gently remind you that actuaries project life *expectancies,* not *guarantees.* In other words—*your* mileage may vary. Don't panic, but please get purposeful. Is whatever you're waiting for worth entirely missing a chosen goal?

Connecting Thoughts:

Do my choices reflect my true priorities? Whose opinion matters most to me and why? If I could let go of anything at this very moment, it would be (...)! Am I stuck somewhere I don't really want to be? Do I really have to stay here?

Your perception of the degrees of intimacy and connection in your life will determine the overall effectiveness of your social experience in intricate and ongoing ways, with a consequential flow-down to health and happiness.

Chapter Four

Tendencies, Transitions, and Limbo-Living

Loneliness is really a matter of perception and choice. How connected do you *feel?*

When self-selected—*Ugh. What a day. Give me silence and bath salts!*—a little isolation can be restorative, particularly for the introvert in need of some processing and decompressing time. Many of us work in professions where we *have* to hibernate a little in order to focus and meet deadlines. Overloaded moms may long for the occasional *solo* bubble bath. *"Look Mommy! My rubber duck is coming in to swim with you!" Splash.*

If unsolicited, however, isolation can lead us into the dark folds of loneliness, stirring up memories of party invitations that didn't arrive and feelings of being the outsider. One of the greatest fears of both young and old is to be forgotten. Many single adults fear dying alone. To be unnoticed and unremembered feels like a judgment on who we are or what we've done. We long to be valued and wanted—particularly during those vulnerable times of transition.

Tendencies: Our Underlying Conditions

Just the Way You Are

Our sensitivity to rejection and the level of need for connection are somewhat of a hardwired individualized predisposition. This DNA-customized *perception* of the degrees of intimacy and connection in your life will determine the overall effectiveness of your social experience in intricate and ongoing ways, with a consequential flow-down to health and happiness. In a 2010 study of twins, Dr. John Cacioppo, Founder and Director of the University of Chicago Center for Cognitive and Social Neuroscience and a pioneer in the field of social neuroscience, gives genetics half the credit—splitting one's likelihood of prolonged and chronic loneliness evenly between an inherited tendency and other environmental factors.[25] An event that plays as a "blip" in one life could stop the whole parade in another.

There are some fixed personality factors impacting when, and if, isolation will grow into loneliness. For instance, our varied landing positions on the introversion/extroversion scale are a pretty good predictor of our initial response to an impromptu party invitation.

Introverts, who have a higher basic rate of arousal to external stimulation, may enjoy the occasional Saturday night out with close friends but could feel overwhelmed at the prospect of back-to-back or large-scale social events. They have to pace themselves. In the words of my friend, Barb, "Most nights, I'm perfectly content to go home to Izzie (her cat) and a good book." A new(er) friend, also named Barb, would consider a weekend with no reason to glam it up a notch or two a wasted opportunity. Both Barbs are wonderfully engaging women, but they have differing levels of need for degrees and types of interaction. Extroverts like Barb II have a lower dopamine response to stimulation in the brain and need more to register "full." For Barb I, that brain reward mechanism tops off pretty quickly and easily. A loaded weekend that energizes one Barb would completely deplete the other Barb's reserves.

It isn't that any of us can't push ourselves in either direction but that we reset and reenergize in specific ways. Try charging an Android phone with an iPhone charger—or vice-versa—it won't work. Similarly, taking an introvert out dancing while she's mourning a breakup won't revive her spirits, and an extrovert may deflate over time if her relationship with a rigidly introverted individual isn't balanced to fit her needs as well.

And then there are us ambiverts, poised in the middle of the introversion/extraversion continuum like tennis champ wannabes anticipating a supersonic serve. We *really really* need to go out and be with people! And, we *really really* need to be alone! And if we move too far into one zone, it tips down like a seesaw, prompting a scramble toward the other end. It can get confusing if you don't understand the yin and yang necessity of *both* needs!

Before I learned this about myself, I feared simple inconsistency. I'd take those "Are You an Introvert/Are You an Extrovert?" surveys and want everything—*"I love parties!" "I love hiding away with a good book,"* because ambiverts comfortably fit into *both* intimate and group situations. We need *both* environments; however, we *need* them when *we* need them! A much-anticipated weekend with friends may feel like a heavy overcoat in August if it immediately follows an extended family vacation. The inordinate solitude of a previous month won't help, because we can't fill this week's need with last week's excess. We need food for hunger and liquid for thirst. We need interaction with others after times of isolation and reflective time after we've had enough stimulation.

The path to isolation and potential loneliness varies from person to person. It will be shorter for some than for others, because it's not just a matter of surrounding yourself with enough people enough of the time. It's about that *feeling* of connection. If it isn't there, being in a big group can feel more like standing alone under a spotlight.

Physical Challenges

Sometimes, a mental or physical condition segregates an individual from easy social access. These body and brain challenges that are beyond our personal control can grow emotionally debilitating as well.

At age 38, my dear friend Adrianne received a devastating multiple sclerosis diagnosis compounded by additional diagnoses and some medical confusion as to what has actually caused her wide-ranging symptoms. She has resolutely forged through myriad medical tests, specialist phone calls and visits, ongoing research, and self-injected medications. "*Yeah, I just kind of fire it into my stomach.*" She has borne the pain and the fear with characteristic spirit, but she grew disheartened as many friends and co-workers succumbed to awkward feelings by ignoring or dismissing her—*although she's quick to point out the outpouring of support from most friends and family members.*

Ignorant comments alternately infuriated or crushed her depending on how her symptoms were impacting a particular day. Two years after ably swimming a half mile across the murky open waters of the Ohio River, Adrianne found herself reluctantly choosing a walker so that she could safely attend her kids' cross-country races. That was a hard day. Sometimes she fights; sometimes she hides. Since her diagnosis, our friendship has required a little extra effort on my part. Not because Adrianne is anything less than a joy to be around, but because she also fights that "I don't want to be a burden" mindset. *Silly girl!*

She'll do this MS (or whatever it is) thing well, because she's buoyant and always finds her way back to *happy.* When she can't "Humvee" her way over an obstacle, we can at least be free with the blunt, "This sucks" statements which has helped her maintain genuine connection.

Me: *(after some bad news) "You, me, and two dozen eggs. We can launch them at one of the trees in my woods. I'll even paint 'MS' on it."*

Adrianne: *(through a mix of laughter and tears) "OK, but we'll have to stand really close!"*

But *how* do you explain, respond, and participate in life when, like Adrianne, you're exhausted and unsure of how well your body will cooperate? Her journey has been a challenging transition for all of us as she fights against easy isolation and creates this new path.

Adrianne is lucky. She was well-connected at the time of her diagnosis and had quite a few friends in the bank, so to speak. Others haven't been so fortunate. During a radio program on isolation and our essential need for connection, I spoke with a couple of housebound callers with long-term disabilities, and they described the excruciating emotional pain of being forever reliant on the varying and fickle initiative of others for social engagement.

"They don't want to deal with (my visual impairment)," said one.

"People don't want to go out of their way to help you," said another.

I don't know their full stories, but it's sadly simple to see how isolation happens in these circumstances. As busy as so many of us are, it's difficult to make room for "one more thing" even if it's potentially life-saving for another. *I'm a little overloaded here at the moment...give me a couple of days to clear some space,* we think. And then, suddenly it's Sunday afternoon, and *Oops. I forgot again.* After a few weeks pass, it's just awkward. We're embarrassed to be "late," not realizing that, for an isolated person, "better late than never" is an acceptable cliché.

I can't fully understand the unique difficulties of disability or disease, but I've contended with shorter periods of physical dependency—and the fear of isolation often overshadowed even the prospect of a painful recovery. Similarly, the desolation of disconnection can be more crippling than the handicap.

Faulty Defaults

Few will argue that some of our natural inclinations are a little off the mark. From that let's-try-something-different dress choice that has never made it out of the closet to the wrong turn you steer into because it's "familiar," bad judgment happens. And over the years, we've developed an internal system of instinctive emotional responses that both help and hurt us. Some of these are related to components of our personalities. You will have a stronger or lesser tendency to push back (or retreat) in response to a perceived affront, and this may vary with different people and even the day. A domineering sister with whom you have a history may elicit a stronger bristling of nerves than a newer friend with similar managerial tendencies. And then there's the pre-caffeinated Monday morning response—*Grrr*—versus the lazy Saturday afternoon reaction—*Whatever.*

Even a smell, tone of voice, or facial expression can evoke unconscious response. For me, the scent of mulled apple cider often prompts a memory of my mother's giant percolating urn next to a plate of Christmas cookies. I remember my visiting grandparents and a lot of happy hopes—a "soft focus" nostalgia that warms gratitude. Similarly, a colleague with a strong resemblance to your dad may tip you toward greater or lesser receptivity, depending on the strength and impact of your daddy/daughter relationship. Sure, you learn to temper the biases you recognize, but you must mentally adjust your swim to factor in the undercurrent.

And then there's the "amygdala hijack,"[26] your personal emergency response system triggered by the genetic "fight or flight" instinct. This reaction is an important safety mechanism for situations where *fully* processing the activating stimuli would shorten your future options. This instinctual internal circuitry works in *milliseconds,* which is great for when you need to, say, sidestep a falling piano. *Hmm...is that a free-falling Steinway directly overhead?* But your fight or flight response can be activated by perceived *emotional* threats to your self-esteem as well. *She ignored me!* With measured intent and practice we can rewire our less than helpful responses to follow more productive paths, but often, we may not even notice that anything's amiss and simply follow our body's lead.

This happens in romantic relationships. It happens in our everyday connection opportunities too. These reactive responses can be so automatic that we don't recognize that they're more about past hurts and habits than the present moment. And inadvertently, we actively perpetuate our own more isolated state.

Transition Points and Other Toe-Stubbers

The barefooted kick to your bedpost. *Made you cringe, didn't I?* You wince. You might release a verbal expression of your discomfort, which has been proven to lessen the pain, by the way—provided your children or mom aren't in earshot.[27]

It's &#%!@! *painful!*

Science agrees with your assessment; stubbing a toe is an extreme encounter for several of your lightly padded nerve ending receptors.[28] These nociceptors quite helpfully blare an instantaneous pain signal to prevent you from inadvertently inflicting further damage to tissue or bone. You're responsive to this message, experiencing no inclination *whatsoever* to rapidly extend your foot in the same direction a second time. You fetch a bandage if needed, slow it down a notch, and give greater respect to floor-level stationary objects for the next several days. But unless you're a real wimp, stubbing your toe is hardly cause for a sick day. *"I'll be out of the office for the remainder of this week. If this is an emergency, please dial my assistant at xxx-xxxx."*

We may do *exactly* that, however, when we bump into painful life experiences. A sick *day?* Many spend *years* waiting for recovery from an abrupt and unwelcome change! The impact reverberates through their ensuing choices, and even their children's lives, diminishing opportunities for joy, both now and in the future—which, contrary to the narrowed perspective, has *not* vanished. It simply revealed itself to be different than expected.

Let's identify and talk about a few of these toe-stubbing transitions that can trip us up because other women—much like you and very near *your* geographic coordinates—are fumbling their way through many of these life-changing events.

Milestones and Detours:

Career

Changes in employment, even when chosen, can be an unwieldy adjustment. Many women have related to me the impact of a career transition on their *non*-working hours. Co-workers provide easy social connection, but when attachment is tied to the workplace, a career setback—or even an advancement—will often repopulate (or depopulate) our opportunities for interaction.

Many office relationships have a workplace perimeter and will not extend beyond a layoff or promotion. These can be friendships of convenience rather than true connections, and losing a job and social connection simultaneously can be overwhelming, deflating, and sobering.

We talked every day—every single Monday through Friday!
But she didn't call me back.

Unvarnished Disclosure: Workplace Perimeter

"I was young and naïve. I really believed we were friends." *Dry laugh.*

When Bridget began working as an associate at a mid-size law firm, "There weren't very many women lawyers. Lynn and I found each other right away and formed what I thought was a decent friendship. We never really talked about work. I guess I was always careful about that. And careful about who I trusted."

The women enjoyed regular lunches. "We'd talk about cooking, our families; you know, good but "safe" stuff. Later, after we both left for better opportunities, we were able to talk about deeper things. Personal matters. Relationships. Her marriage."

"It ended up that there were three of us—Lynn, me, and a third woman Amy, who still worked at the firm. We kept connected for a short time and even traveled together. Had a *blast* on trips to Phoenix and Vegas."

And then, it faded away.

"I guess the two of them had a more common life experience. You know, married with kids. Over time, I kind of just slid out of the picture."

It hurt.

"I was more careful in my next job. Kept my distance a little more. And then when I got married, to an admittedly poor choice of man, I felt like a pariah! My 'friends' at *that* firm quickly began to distance themselves from me."

When she finally left the firm, there weren't really any friendships to carry forward.

Over time, Bridget has grown more and more cautious in trusting workplace friendships. "They're 'work' friends. It doesn't really seem to transfer outside the office."

I asked about her current job in a third law firm.

"I talk to Beth a lot. My secretary. That's about it."

Location

The same goes for neighbors. That easy end-of-the-driveway camaraderie may fade when you aren't sharing power tools and your distaste of the unkempt corner lot. Real connections can make the move with you—*particularly if you move just across town to a home with an in-ground pool.* But often the *new* neighbor is equally amenable to driveway chats and has just as strong and viable an opinion on what the homeowners' association should do to maintain property values. You're replaceable.

Even when the big move is an upgrade in terms of square footage and amenities, it is likely to be accompanied by the pressures of an upsized mortgage. The happy homeowners still need to unpack boxes, learn new routines, revamp logistics, and agree on a new "best" carryout pizza. There's more to clean, more to maintain, and more responsibilities to negotiate with a partner or delegate to hired help. Even a dream house can keep you up at night and will potentially cut into the time and energy required to build friendships in the new location.

Shame and Humiliation

Tanya and her husband made the evening news—and the internet—in a damning video that included freezable frames of both their home address and surname. A dramatic 911 call from a concerned neighbor led to a police raid, handily captured by a local news crew. The sensationalistic TV coverage, including a transcription of the phone call and video of deputies removing boxes of purported evidence from her husband's alleged marijuana growing operation, ensured maximum impact.

The headline story provided enough details for her community to fill in the spaces and spread the news. Although Tanya proclaimed herself an innocent spouse, no one seemed to care what she did or didn't know. She kept her husband but lost her job, her social identity, and many of her hopes for the future. Even worse, with Facebook but a click away, she had easy access to all of the humiliating gossip and innuendo. Friends vanished, but so did Tanya—her shame enlarging and reinforcing the barrier created by the fallout from the explosive scandal.

Author Jon Ronson describes social media as a "stage for constant artificially high dramas." "Everybody's either a magnificent hero or a sickening villain." He compares us to would-be amateur detectives, searching out "inherent evil" in others.[29]

Mom's *"Stop crossing your eyes—your face will freeze like that!"* has evolved into the *"Online is forever"* warning we give our kids as we breathe silent thanks that our *own* "paper trails" truly *were* made of biodegradable wide-ruled notebook filler.

It's effortless to join the virtual crowd. With a tweet or comment, we can align ourselves with the "good guys." You're only throwing your two cents in, right? But as Tanya quickly discovered, that can add up to a lot of loose change when you're on the receiving end. As a society, it seems we're alarmingly quick to rally—and to exclude. And by the time *everyone* weighs in, the scale of justice is often tipped on its side.

A social media shunning amplifies shame to infinity and can blast the target right out of society into an isolation that's hard to escape. Or even want to escape. Tanya still struggles.

Death or Extended Illness

A miscarriage, the overdose death of a teen, or the diagnosis of a chronic condition can pull us away from healing connections. And often, extended isolation is but one more diminishment after the death of a spouse.

When "happily ever after" dissolves to a blank screen, the surviving spouse can be at a loss for even the next footstep. The rest of us are helpless to fully understand the massive impact of permanently losing a life partner too soon. The good intentions of concerned friends may be buried beneath the awkwardness of uncomfortable feelings, and any preceding period of illness can be the push-off for a slow drift from connection.

My sister, who lost her first husband to lung cancer when she was in her early forties, remembers a couple of dog-walking neighbors who would receive sudden text messages, requiring their full attention, whenever they neared her or her husband, Greg. Lacking the "right words," these neighborhood friends chose no words at all. *Or quite possibly, they were preoccupied by their own undisclosed challenges—it happens.* As Greg's eventual death neared, friends and family engulfed her, but as is often the case, after the post-funeral house tasks were completed, most ebbed away. She eventually found a widows' support group and was gradually able to build forward as she came to terms with her deep loss. But she retreated from view many times—tugged back only by that deeply empathetic group, a good therapist, and the support of her family and a few persistent friends.

A surviving spouse unable to adjust to this excruciating life transition will often decline both physically and emotionally. Solid social connections are essential. *Quality* of life will significantly diminish if the *value* ascribed to its remainder is emotionally downgraded. If not proactive, widows and widowers can very easily be isolated by their own unique experience with grief. The situational loneliness can develop into a chronic condition from which the surviving spouse never truly heals.

Divorce

Divorce is, unfortunately, an increasingly common detour. With extended life spans and better late life health, some couples who latched on to one another in youth or—as with many second or third marriages—during a time of great need, find that forever isn't worth the emotional price tag. Whether a marriage's end sparks revelation and growth into a better self, is a destructive tear-down of dreams, or lands you somewhere in between—these endings pause our momentum. The division of assets at marital end almost always downsizes the friend list through either a tacit apportionment—*"Thank God, I don't have to sit through anymore of those 'you had to be there' college-buddy stories"*—or the rapid retreat of intact couples fearing a contagion.

And beyond that basic attrition, there's the ramp-up time on sorting and reassembling the pieces after the whole blanket toss. It's hard! On the other side of domestic court, single parents often find themselves journeying across an oddly jarring landscape: mountains of busyness during their "kid times," surrounded by a vast, sterile kid-free wilderness. In the latter, they must frantically make camp for themselves and the tribe, catch up on hunting and gathering—chasing down all the essentials for the kids' eventual return—and wash a week's worth of laundry before the next mountaintop experience. Hot and cold. Feast and famine. *How do you dress for that?!*

Embarrassment, exhaustion, bewilderment...feelings like these don't motivate sociability.

New Life Stages—More and Less Responsibility

And then sometimes, an "emptied nest" really is, well, empty. All those years of raising kids while pursuing a career and maintaining a marriage and household didn't leave much time for building more than your basic carpool-based support system, did it? When those family-style dinners are subsequently downsized to a table for two, the spotlight can quickly focus on the one chewing noisily in the point position. Similar to shining a flashlight on one spot in a cave—the darkness can be vast, but our focus is limited to what is lit up directly in front of us.

Retirement can have a similar effect. For some, it's a finish line of sorts. But, once you grab your medal, then what? Breakfast, lunch, *and* dinner with the noisy chewer?

Discontent can thud heavily on the marital relationship, but often the sadness is part of a much larger issue of *overall* isolation in the midst of this significant life transition. Incidentally, spouses who expect one another to be problem solvers—*"Fix my life!"*—rather than fellow sojourners, can find an easy target for their unhappiness but are likely to rinse and repeat their way through more misery unless they first shine that spotlight on their own feet. A divorce or a romantic attachment outside the marriage will merely add to the complexity of solving the issue of an overall disconnection.

Caring for older parents and/or grandparents can also isolate us.

When my parents died just beyond age sixty and within five months of one another—leaving my sisters and me to care for three grandparents in addition to raising our own families—I had no understanding of our heightened stress levels until the waters receded ten years later. By then, my marriage had ended, and my children were growing into that stage where they simultaneously needed *more*—driving, listening, coaching, feeding—and *less* from me.

*"It's like this. You're a cool mom, but you're still **my** mom. Can you pull-eeze not talk to me in front of my friends!"* -My daughter Hannah, age 13

In the meantime, I'd fallen into a system of trading lingering stress for the newest yearly model and had isolated myself to be a caretaker of everyone except myself—segueing effortlessly from crazy-busy mom to crazy-busy mom with sick parents to crazy-busy, divorced mom grieving her parents while aiding ailing grandparents. When my last grandparent died as I held her hand on Thanksgiving Day in 2010, I felt completely lost. Grandma Dugan had been my go-to when I didn't know where else to go. She had been a friend who needed me, and I needed to be needed. Like many, I'd honed my focus to the detriment of overall balance.

Shifting a kid-focused or caregiving existence to a build-my-*own* life mindset is a huge challenge for many of us. Most busy moms haven't had time to consider what life might include beyond what was initially mandated by school, sports practices, music lessons, household maintenance, and work schedules.

Friends may have been essential to maintaining the pace, but friend*ships* often remained undeveloped, relegated to "we should have coffee sometime." We saved them for *someday,* never dreaming there would actually be a day we wouldn't be surprised by a last-minute need for poster board or a clean soccer uniform.

"Oh, and after you blow-dry my jersey, Coach said we're in charge of snacks this week."

"Mom, can you even hear me with your hands over your ears like that?"

The level of relief one feels in the downsizing of deadlines will measure directly against what is waiting in the wings. Ideally, there are already some supportive friends in the program, but if you, like me, spent the equivalent of four months quick-thawing dinners in the microwave, it's more likely been a one-woman show.

It's no wonder there's an echo in the evening!

Shifting Social Connection Zones

While our *need* for connection remains constant, the means of finding and building those friendships will vary during or following a major transition. Our own desire and ability to engage with others may waver a bit when confronted with what we perceive to be a downturn. Self-assurance get a little dinged up? You might not feel like your life is quite up for company.

"Put my best foot forward"? Can we at least wait until I have both of them on the ground again?

As a five-year-old, all you had to do was be the girl with the jump rope to make a new friend. It's a lot harder as a hesitant thirty-, forty-, or fifty-something who has had her fair share of rejection and regret. Younger You hadn't been jaded by betrayals, competitiveness, and discourtesies. By midlife, however, we've bumped into a few of Life's "uglies," and we may have a finely-tuned, disappointment avoidance system. When you *switch* social connection zones, getting the lay of the land can be intimidating, and we often revert to old habits that may or may not have been effective before and simply don't fit where we are today.

In the beginning, mom may have directed most of your socialization. "Honey, this is Mrs. Morris and her daughter, Amanda. Why don't you girls go outside and play on the swing set?" *That question mark is only an acknowledgement of the word "why." In actuality mom's "suggestion" was usually a declarative sentence.*

The mom-selected friends were usually fine and definitely one-upped having to explain the pile of clothes under the bed. And, there was usually a "because we have company" snack upgrade included, right? While these pairings were often driven by one mom's affinity for another—*"We should get together for coffee. How old is your daughter?"*—there was at least a steady supply of friend options from mom, in the neighborhood, and at school.

And then there were the built-ins: our siblings. The varying dynamics of these mandated-by-mom-and-dad relationships were likely to impact our approach to the world at large for at least a few years. Brothers provided first views of the male species—*"Ew, gross! Mom, make him close his mouth when he's eating!"*—at both its best and worst. Sisters...well, we have definite opinions and attitudes about our sisters. *"She's my best friend,"* or *"We haven't spoken in three years."*

A pivotal moment arrived when we began to choose our own friends: a neighbor or classmate, or maybe a fellow tortured soul in beginner's swimming class. Often it was a proximate choice—it was easier to befriend more available neighbor kids—but sometimes, it was illogical. A random playground connection prompted a DIY friendship, just because...

Making those early friendship choices meant we had begun forming and acting upon preferences. We knew enough about who we were becoming to recognize and appreciate personality clicks. These chosen connections didn't always fit within the reasonable reach of mom's station wagon, but that they existed at all was indicative of a budding self-awareness and a modicum of maturity. And it was pretty simple—often all you had to do was start playing. Get in the four-square or tetherball line. Walk up to the swings. Join the crowd gathering for an impromptu backyard game of Kickball, Spud, or Ghost-in-the-Graveyard.

Many of the women I interviewed tied important childhood memories to pint-sized people. They remembered the joyous freedom of wheeling through the neighborhood on a bike to meet a friend at a park or family home. With our early friends, we began to build our own worlds and have experiences separate from what mom and dad had created for us. While our first environments certainly varied, for most of us there existed a sort of kid universe filled with a galaxy's worth of other children at least close to our own ages.

For some of us, however, it got progressively harder. More complicated. By middle and high school, many of us felt like a Noxzema-scented web of exposed nerves—tentative and vulnerable to raging hormones and underlying social currents. The protocol and options for friend-finding had changed. There were unspoken rules for everything from lunch table seating to whom you said "hi" to in the hallways. It was a caste system of sorts, and few had the confidence to simply ignore it.

It was an awkward, often treacherous zone where friends dropped us—or, shamefully, we ourselves upgraded for more popular girls. There was awareness that at least some of our friendships were commodities useful to our navigation through puberty into young adulthood. Establishing a personal identity within the social hierarchy amidst differing rates of emotional and physical development was fraught with angst, missteps, and tension. Those early betrayals, geographic disruptions, and outright rejections were sometimes soul-crushing blows which altered our whole approach to friend-making. Our friends were essential to developing our relational self. We liked them, even loved them, but we also needed them very much, whether we could admit this or not.

College and early career experiences opened up new social geographic zones. You might have traded your parents' home for a university community or accepted a job with career-launching contemporaries in another city or state. Within this zone, we're often *deluged* with potential connections. Surrounded by peers with similar interests, the pools of possible romantic partners and potential friends seemed endless. Time stretched ahead on a wide horizon, and while you might have been aware of a few fading friendships, your level of connection seemed like something you could always turn on when you really needed it, like tap water.

At some point, you might have chosen a life partner and begun identifying yourself as part of a family with kids, "couple friends," and a neighborhood or church community. While even the happy events—new homes, promotions, and babies—tracked a little stress into our lives, those transitions had obvious upsides. We juggled, but it was juggling with a sense of hopeful purpose.

But as life hit full stride with family and career and financial responsibilities, we also began to experience more loss—death, divorce, career and financial setbacks—the hard and hurtful transitions we'd prefer to view on a big screen with fistfuls of popcorn. It was more gratifying to add the happy possibilities represented by children and accelerating careers. But now that your mouthy teen needs braces, your husband needs a new resume—ASAP, because layoffs are imminent—and Mom's hip is acting up, it may feel like you traded your ascent toward "happily ever after" for a bumpy ride on the Dow Jones chart.

Within this stage of life, we begin to feel a need for real connection with people who know and care about us, but for many, it suddenly appears that the pool of potential friends has evaporated—just when we finally need them in a real way.

Many awaken in their thirties or forties with an alarming sense of "I missed it!"—meaning that small youth-sized window through which we were to gather lifelong friendships to carry us through adulthood. We were lost in our own insecurities or focused on our own footing, and the window seemingly closed behind us. Additional transitions hit like waves when our feet aren't yet set for them. Defensively, we fight further movement, abruptly realizing that there are more route-changing variables than we originally recognized and that we have less control over our journey than we had hoped and believed.

Transition Zone Trouble

My oldest son Zak has compared some of our family vacation adventures to boot camp—not the "No AC in the beach house" version of challenging, but the kind where we disengage from the outside world with backpacks and turkey jerky and emerge as bonded specimens of fitness. *Admittedly, as I've blipped past fifty, my definition of "specimen" is on a sliding scale, but I'm fighting the good fight and occasionally have the blisters and broken fingernails to prove it.* Many of these adventures have launched from remote trailheads in Colorado.

Because we do *not* want to be featured in a local news mountain rescue story, I do a lot of preparation. We have appropriate gear, know our limits, and I give the kids a pre-trip reminder that helicopter rescues from mountains run to about five hundred dollars per person. While we're partial to strenuous treks, we're non-technical climbers—*with a preference for hot showers and comfortable beds at the end of the day, thank you very much*—so we stick to Class 2 trail routes, so designated by factors such as distance, terrain, and elevation change. Altitude gains bring fluctuations in weather and temperature, which in turn generate the variations in terrain, vegetation, and wildlife that transform a scenic hike into a true adventure.

We often begin these treks in a montane region characterized by forests of Ponderosa pine, Douglas fir, or shimmering aspen trees before segueing into flowered sub-alpine meadows with occasional stands of pine at around 10,000 feet. We finally venture above the tree-line at around 11,500 feet and finish our ascents well into the alpine zone.

You'll note that I used "around" in describing the geological zone shifts. That's because there is always a bit of space between these proximate biospheres where the environment kind of works out what it's going to be. This land where the shift between ecological zones occurs is characterized by so-called environmental tension[30]—*"I think I'm a forest, but I have these meadow moments...I'm so conflicted!"*—with critters from bordering zones intermingling a bit and dwarfed pines giving it the old college try until the altitude casts a conclusive ruling. *"I said sub-alpine, and that's final!"*

The contrasts can be extreme. As we step nimbly and numbly through ice fields, traverse frigid burbling streams, and scramble over boulders up the steep trails of these mountain peaks, we're alternately zipping up jackets and pulling hats down over our ears only to peel off those layers, and more, when exertion reheats and begins to bake us—and yanking those same layers out of our packs yet again when a chill sets in. *The wardrobe changes are part of the family bonding fun and provide my children a peek into the adventures of menopause.*

There is continuous change: in the environment and beauty around us, in our bodies and minds, in the altitude, weather, and view, and in our overall perspective. There is exhilaration in this contrast and in the knowing that we are pushing against our supposed limits, perhaps stretching them just a bit further. And the swell of joy and sense of accomplishment when the mountaintop goal is achieved—revealing the splendor of a summit view—is unparalleled.

Oh, that we could so hopefully and happily travel from one *life* zone into the next.

But most of us don't. Were the transition of a divorce or an unwelcome relocation a purely geographic ecological event, many of us would plop down on a boulder in that transition zone, muttering, "I don't *want* to wear a jacket. I never had to put a jacket on when I was married/employed/a hands-on mom. I don't know *how* to put *on* this jacket! And a hat?! You've got to be kidding me. I don't look good in hats—just let me go back to where I didn't *need* a jacket or hat or anything I haven't used before!"

Many of us carry a mental map of our life journey-to-be and react with disbelief, panic, and/or deep disappointment when we spot a "Road Closed" sign in front of the chosen route.

"Divorce? But we were going to live happily ever after and retire to a beach house after the kids graduate and . . ."

"He can't be fired just like that! We've got a mortgage and a kid in college!"

While even our most significant transitions are fairly common, they land—*often with a thud*—outside what we've experienced to that point and can easily trip us up. Suddenly, we find ourselves at the edge of a new and unfamiliar life zone that will require some mental and physical adjustments. Once we actively participate in the transition, we can, and many times do, find joy in the new normal, but frequently, we don't even *want* to adjust. We're stuck and agape at the strangeness of it. Or the "not fair" aspect—i.e., *"This isn't what I ordered!"* We're focused on a now unavailable option, behind or before us, and stymied by the apparent block to our intended path. The *original* ending still captivates us. Our eyes fixate on the demarcation, that point in time when everything "changed," diminishing all potential alternatives to inferior substitutes for what was planned.

While grieving our more momentous, undesirable changes is an essential part of the healing process, stalling there indefinitely, hoping for a way back, will only extend the misery. Most of these significant life zone transitions are one-way. We *can't* go back. Surly teens don't "ungrow" their way back to sweet-voiced toddlers; we can't move back into the *Sold!* family home. Changes to age and address are inevitable, but change is *always* a stress to our sense of equilibrium.

A transition is often a fundamental definitional change to identity. The recently unemployed may struggle to introduce herself without sharing a job description. The former *wife* and mother must now identify as a single mom. With the death of parents, a woman is no longer a daughter. And a severe financial setback is likely to impact social and community affiliations, straining or severing previous connection points.

Even the inevitable, "should have seen that coming" segues of life can create drag on our momentum. Switching the first digit of our age as we broach a new decade, for instance...How much of *your* valuable energy drained into the drama of turning thirty, forty, or fifty? And parents who have spent a couple of decades thoughtfully building confidence and independent-thinking into their offspring can have significant difficulty with some of the confident, independent choices these same children make, forgetting that the echo in a quieted, empty house is actually a "Good job, Mom!" and an "I can take it from here, Dad!"

Intellectually, this makes no sense, which would be great if intellect actually got the steering wheel for all of our decision-making. But alas, women teeter around on crippling 5-inch heels, hopeful balding men comb over thin strands of sparse hair, and most of us engage in some magical thinking and/or sit frozen on a "pause" button beside these unexpected obstructions that might better be better viewed as detours.

Limbo-Living and Chronic Loneliness

We'll cover some effective strategies for weathering transitions in Section Three, but it's important to recognize the impact they can and do have on social connection. Until you get the lay of the land in a new life zone—say, the high school mom zone as you begin the transition toward an emptied nest, or the caregiving zone where you may no longer be able to lightly socialize with neighbors—you will feel fairly isolated and maybe even a bit lonely. Those in your immediate vicinity may not be able to relate to the new parameters of your life, and disconnection can occur fairly easily.

Often this is unavoidable. There are less easy opportunities for contact. And you may not feel like talking with old acquaintances who simply can't relate to your life as it now stands. But this is a critical fork, from which you can begin to move in a new direction, creating new friendships, or you can stay rooted as your connections further dwindle. The first choice will move you from a "situational loneliness" precipitated by a turn of events or change of life back into healthy connection. The second option is a step toward "chronic loneliness" via what I've come to call "limbo-living."

Situational loneliness can stifle joy for a while, limbo-living devalues it, and chronic loneliness is, ultimately, a joy killer.

Situational Loneliness: A temporary disconnection, often occurring during a time of transition, that can either deepen our gratitude for relationship, allowing us to reaffirm the value of connection, or begin to immobilize and more permanently isolate us.

Limbo-Living: A state of existing rather than participating in one's own life while waiting for circumstances or people to change.

Chronic Loneliness: A self-perpetuating condition of a disconnected life that causes physical and emotional harm.

While the temporary situational loneliness sometimes created by career changes, long illnesses, and changes to relationship status is often unavoidable, without care, these crises can unfortunately become real dead-ends for previously connected individuals. A boulder-sitting breather can extend into a stagnating standstill at the edge of a new and unfamiliar life zone. Adults, severed from one life or lifestyle and not fully grafted into the next, can easily slide into limbo-living as they passively wait for "new" to begin instead of striding forward to meet it. Loneliness can then become a chronic condition, a way of life that can be very difficult to change.

It's understandable for your brain to "toss its neurons" when negative stimuli overwhelm. It can be hard enough just choosing amongst good options! When the answers all have degrees of discomfort attached to them—*assisted living or home care for Dad?* —it can feel like you're psyching yourself for a reach-and-grab from hot coals. Not surprisingly, we often opt to pull our arms in, wrap them tightly around our middle—*or an ice cream spoon or the TV remote*—and sit on our chosen boulder.

But here's the word from a woman who tried the extended-stay option in a few of my transition zones: My limbo-living extended the wrong part of my life journey. It was like checking into a funky-smelling hotel room and resignedly flipping on the closed-circuit TV rather than exploring other options. Nothing got better until I moved. Furthermore, *every single challenge*—from a life-threatening illness with one of my children to an international legal case with my last book—grew something new inside of me that has been exceptionally useful in my journey forward from that point. My daughter's frightening battle against anorexia eventually birthed a strong and empathetic young woman, gifted with both words and wisdom. Our family relationships deepened as we all endured and survived the pain, eventually landing up to our ears in gratitude. Once I grasped the extent of the legal battle I faced and moved from panicked paralysis into action mode, I learned how to research and write a legal brief and won the case. *Not on my bucket list, but I'll check it off, nonetheless!* The pivotal point has always been my intentional shift from panic to purposeful choice.

There is inherent tension and stress in moving from the familiar toward the blank, undefined space ahead of us. And there is an understandable instinct to dig in our heels and hold onto what we already know and feel better equipped to handle. Even when everything flips, and the road back to Kansas has been wiped out by the twister, evil witch, *and* all those nasty flying monkeys, we want to go back! We want to click those ruby slippers and time-travel back to black and white.

But once you do finally slide off your boulder and take your first steps forward into the next life zone, you begin an acclimation process. Yes, it's different, but it's *yours.* And it can be your choice to begin exploring the unique aspects of your new surroundings and to grow the connections that will make it more than just livable.

Often, these transitions will grow valuable wisdom and perspective within us. We find that as we strained and stretched to overcome the challenge of our change, new skills and strengths were mined that we've now added to our personal assets column. Yes, the view is changed, but it reveals a different sort of beauty, and one that we can actually enjoy if we allow ourselves to do so. *And your alternative is . . .?*

"Unfair" happens to *everyone. Nobody* likes it. But we all have to deal with our personalized allotments. Dead-ends, detours, and even off-the-map moments are not aberrations but should be expected as tweaks to our travel. It's too bad we don't have a mental GPS to reassure us on the updated itinerary. *Recalculating... recalculating...* but absent the cushioning layers of contentment, a painful transition can often be your *best* opportunity to build more meaningful, reality-based connections.

Connection Point

Can you see where it happened? The disconnect? Were you able to identify some of the reasons behind your current isolation?

Is the fact of your disconnection now a little more understandable?

I began to feel a *lot* better about myself once I understood that my loneliness was the predictable result of numerous factors, many of which were beyond my immediate control. Low self-confidence and a misunderstanding of the importance of female friends, combined with a busy family life, disintegrating marriage, and family deaths...it's no wonder I found myself in a sad and friendless space! By identifying its multiple causes, I could finally see that isolation was a completely understandable effect—*not* a personal failing. I could also begin looking for factors I could change. I wasn't a bad, weird, or boring person. Just an awfully lonely one.

What brought you to this place? Chances are that a combination of personal tendencies and transition points all contributed toward your disconnection. Whether you're a recent empty-nester or widow; whether you've relocated for a spouse's job or for your own career; whether this current isolation feels strange or all too familiar—it's important you see it for what it is: an outcome, but not an ending.

Remember those dot-to-dot pictures of your childhood? They didn't look like much until you mastered the alphabet or numerical order and began connecting the little circles, did they? Think of yourself as a currently unconnected dot, surrounded by unlimited points of connection that can develop into any picture you wish to create. That's powerful! Maybe you were once happily connected into another picture, and some—or all—of those lines have been erased or blurred. That's unfortunate, but it's time to start looking for your new connections and to begin creating a new vision for the life still ahead of you.

Connecting Thought:

Now that I can begin to see how this isolation happened and understand that a lack of friends doesn't mean I'm unlikeable, I can be open to constructive solutions. I don't like this disconnected place, but it could have happened to anyone faced with my set of circumstances. I feel lonely because I am disconnected, and this can be fixed!

SECTION TWO

Focus on Friendship

"I look around the table at all these women and see both 'where I was' and 'where I want to be.'"

Chapter Five

My Cabernet Coaches

Ugh. Life can be kind of a mess sometimes. It's amazing how far off-track we can get when we're simply scurrying to keep up. Many of us raced off toward one emergency, only to get distracted by the next...until we lost sight of making actual choices about how to spend our time and energy. And those little (and big) life emergencies don't exactly line up single file for us, do they? They're more like the cars in rush-hour traffic, squeezing in and cutting us off, *while leaning on the horn and elevating a single digit to express displeasure at our inability to anticipate their obvious priority status.*

Throw in a life transition—or two, or three—and it's no wonder we occasionally feel detached from the life we're currently enrolled in.

But I bet you have already quietly pondered or steadfastly ignored your separation. *I* certainly did. My own disconnection pressed in for *years* before I was able to take a deep breath and confront it head on.

The soundtrack to *My Best Friend's Wedding* was in frequent play during my Mom Commute years. Anyone who has road-warriored that rigorous, finely-tuned and timed route between schools, practices, meets, games, performances, and other assorted events comprehends the adrenaline-laced atmosphere. *"Mom, I* ***can't*** *be late again!" "Why does* **he** *get dropped off first?!" "Who's driving me home again?"* Happy music helped—*as did a "windows down" rule if shin guards had not been hermetically odor-sealed beneath a thick layer of freshly laundered socks.* We'd merrily sing along to the upbeat tunes, and the kids would adjust to the inconveniences presented by their siblings' concurrent schedules.

One such afternoon, Hannah asked me with charming naiveté from which friend's wedding the music had come. Cute, huh? I explained that it was actually just the title of an old Julia Roberts movie. We laughed and sang a little more. And then she continued, "I've been trying *all this time* to figure out who it could be! One of your sisters, or maybe someone I don't know...you don't do anything with Rhonda or Nancy anymore. Who *is* your best friend, Mommy?"

I remember my heart kind of sinking as I soft-pedaled my way to an answer that would *not* include an explanation of the post-divorce friend exodus and my basic lack of connection. I went with the broad-stroked, "I guess I just prefer having *lots* of friends to only *one* best friend, honey. And it's been *sooo* busy lately! I guess I haven't had much time for anybody! Oh—our favorite song is next!" I was kind of embarrassed. I was sad that no one liked me—*or more truthfully, that no one really* ***knew*** *me.*

But I didn't know how to fix it. I didn't know if it was even fixable! Maybe I'd missed that boat—like the new kid starting school a couple of months after the first-day desk assignments. Everyone had already picked out their friends. There wasn't room for anyone who obviously wasn't one of the cool kids. I was simply Heather: an under-confident, 40-something mom of three, struggling to rebuild her life after a horrendous three-year divorce. That sort of pedigree doesn't generate many lunch table invitations.

That heavy humiliation still enfolded my ongoing isolation a couple of years later when Hannah, once again, asked about my non-existent friends. "Remember when I thought that music was from *your* best friend's wedding, Mommy?" We laughed. "Who is your best friend *now*, Mommy?"

Again, I deflected. The honest non-kid friendly answer would have been: "I don't have any friends, Hannah. There are other very sad songs on that soundtrack that I skip when you're in the car. I save those for the long drives home after I've dropped you off at your dad's. There are whole weekends when my phone never rings, and the only voice I hear is my own, talking to Lily [our dog]. What friends I *hoped* I had disappeared when I went through with the divorce filing. *I thought I was divorcing your dad, not my whole life!* I try to keep busy. I go on long bike rides, pretending I actually prefer to be alone, but those are long, dark weekends. My own family ignores me. In the darkest moments, I wonder what I would do if you kids weren't here to compel my next steps. I go on dates sometimes, and I'm hoping the next guy will be the magical missing piece that will fill in all the gaps and be my lifetime love. It just takes one, you know...*Sigh*. But friends? I wouldn't have any idea where to find one."

I knew better than to speak those words to my daughter, but I didn't understand how important it would be to speak them to myself. When you have faint hope of catching up, you quickly lose any sense of urgency. It can be hard to take even that first step.

I had a *lot* of excuses. Here are a handful:

I'm too busy. *Seriously. I'll worry about "me" in twenty years—after my kids are launched and I've caught up on laundry.*

Other people are already too busy living the life I had hoped for. *Look at them...***She** *has my life plus a marriage. And* **(Other) She** *has an exciting but demanding job and makes actual plans with real friends for her weekends.*

I'm boring. *What can I offer? Netflix has more variety, more depth, and is available on demand. I'm just available. Really, really available . . .*

My life is too messy. *How could I even begin? I'm behind on* **everything***. For fun, my daughter and niece sometimes search for the oldest expiration dates in my pantry with bonus points for anything predating my youngest son. You have a junk drawer? I have a junk basement and an embarrassing garage, and don't even get me started on the divorce.*

It's too hard to plan ahead. *Again, where will I put you?*

I don't want to impose on anyone. *Your life is far more interesting. I'm wearing boots because my socks don't match.*

I don't know how. *Can't someone just, I don't know...notice the yearning in my heart? Do I really have to spell it out?*

It's too awkward. *I hated being the new kid in middle school, and I hate it even more here in so-called middle age! Then, there was only the (significant) danger of embarrassing myself. Now, I'm a "plus three." Embarrassments with teenagers in the vicinity have exponential factors I don't even want to calculate.*

It's too late. *I'm half of a defunct couple. None of our old friends want a partial set, and all of the single people paired off into their friend groups already.*

But when I finally bottomed out at the end of a two-year relationship and was in desperate agony over a guy that I'd, frankly, been trying to escape, I found my new beginning.

You see, my depression kind of knocked all the excuses down. Finally—*Hallelujah!*—I couldn't just pile up the rubble to jerry-rig a new wall. My choices came down to A) continuing what obviously wasn't working for me, or B) trying something new.

Ending Inertia

While identifying the need became easier—*kind of like walking into an empty house and saying, "Hmm...needs furniture"*—working out how to fill the void and begin changing my life proved a little harder. Hopefully, some of the things I finally learned will save *you* a few steps.

Inertia was my oh-so-easy default, but it's a non-choice that boils down to simple risk avoidance. You can't make a navigational error if you don't move, right? You can't stub your toe, twist your ankle, or fall off the side of a cliff if you never extend your foot in a new direction. If you don't actually try to reach out to others, no one can ignore you, forget you, or reject you.

This is a completely understandable response, but it's a survival mechanism gone bad—the equivalent of standing on a mountaintop during a lightning storm with your fingers in your ears.

Inertia says, "I don't know what to do next" and "Is it really worth it?" Sometimes it says, "This isn't fair, and I'm not moving until it changes." But it will ultimately narrow your future options. If something *isn't* "fair" and you've *already* lost a few options, to further reduce your available opportunities doesn't make a lot of sense, does it?

Maintaining the status quo requires little more than a slight flip of the fin, but treading water is a postponement of active choice and will gradually drain energy you could be using as forward momentum. *It's the equivalent of sitting in your car on the side of the road and revving your engine when you're already low on gas.*

While there *are* exhausted moments in which even choosing dinner off of a restaurant menu feels complex, making choices is an *adult navigational responsibility*. Establishing a plan with which to advance from isolated misery to somewhere you can begin building your own happiness is a bold move, but it's a *grownup* decision with sizeable benefits. It's a step from the sideline to the playing field. And by now we all have to focus on moving our own ball.

Merging your life with the lives of those around you requires a little momentum—you have to stoke your own engine a little and develop a deeper awareness of others. Many of those "busy" people around you—aren't. They're practicing that timeless tactic of avoidance.

You mean I'm not the only one feeling this way?

Not by a long shot.

Merging into social connection will require some planning and a decision on direction. It requires a "No More!" mentality. Can you muster this?

How is that island thing working for you?

That was a rhetorical question, btw.

We need each other. Truly. We all need friends.

Face the Space

With a bare-faced view of my own reality—*You don't have any real friends, Heather.*

"But—"

Hold on. You really need to hear this Heather. Not a single ONE!

I could no longer ignore it. Well, I guess I *could* have. *Hum de dum, let's go clean another closet . . .*

But truly, I was sick and tired of being sick and tired of my life. Once I could identify what the root issue was—*not* my lack of a love relationship, but rather my lack of *any* significant relationships—I knew I had to figure something out, or it was going to be a long haul to the retirement home.

This is the first step for any of us. We have to face the space. Before you can begin finding solutions, you have to get motivated by the problem itself. You have to quantify a difficult and painful situation: "I'm isolated." "I'm lonely." "I wish I had solid and meaningful friendships."

Otherwise, you'll keep avoiding it. *C'mon, you know you will. Just like that rather scary accumulation under the fridge.* It's icky. Unattractive. If we don't look closely, it's almost like it isn't there—except for that nagging sadness *(and those shriveled peas)*. Speaking these words aloud so that you can really hear them is a necessary first step.

So, if this is you, say it aloud: "I'm lonely. I need to find some friends. I want more for my life and don't want to live this way any longer."

Go back to the last paragraph if your lips didn't move. You've got to hear this from your own heart! It's difficult to face these facts, but we can't begin to change them until we've defined them. Read these next questions—discuss them with your book club group, your dog, or with yourself, but really consider them. It's important that you write down your answers or speak them aloud to give them form. Be honest. I have, and now it's your turn. *OK. You can continue talking to yourself in your head if you can't find a pen, but please! Listen to your answers.*

Is there anyone you could comfortably call for no reason at all?
Who would be genuinely thrilled for *your* good fortune if you were given a free "dream vacation?"
Do you ever get calls from non-telemarketers soliciting your opinion?
Can you think of three people you could ask for help if you had car trouble or a surgery?
Who do you get together with on a regular basis to talk about the big and little things of life?
If your kids wanted to celebrate you, what non-family members would receive invitations?
Who knows you well enough to say, "This reminded me of you"?
Are these questions making you anxious or sad? *Hang in there—you're doing great. Pre-Cabernet Coaches, I'd have closed this book and distracted myself with Facebook by now.*
To which non-family members could you say, "Come on over" and not have to give an address?
Was there a time in your life you could have answered these questions differently?
Do you want to change some of these answers?

Let me add this: You *can* change the majority of your answers! While looking for a teleport back to some era behind your back is non-productive, it's OK to hope for a more connected life—because we can make that happen!

Straight from My Cabernet Coaches

If you haven't experienced real connection in a while, you may have forgotten how good it feels to be woven into something bigger than your own up-and-down life. We'll expand on some of these later but allow me to briefly elaborate on a few benefits of good friendship as shared with me by women just like you.

1) Refreshment.

Our Wednesday night happy hour gatherings are an essential reset for many of us. I think we could clink coffee cups and achieve similar results—*except we'd inevitably get deep into conversation and be late for morning meetings which would completely mess with the stress-free zone we've established.* By the time the midweek mark rolls into view, Friday's end-of-week checklist lies directly ahead, along with the realization that it somehow grew a bit longer between Monday and Tuesday. And yet, despite these constraints, the Wednesday night pause can be very conducive to overall productivity. Connection unscrews the valve we tighten around burgeoning stress, allowing its release as laughter with sympathetic friends rather than an angry and inappropriate blow up at work or home.

> *"I didn't want to leave! The conversations were so good. My soul needed that. Thank you, Heather for being our lead coach and coordinator extraordinaire."*
>
> -Cabernet Coach Kris N.

Yeah, my name is in there, but that really *isn't* about me. All I did was create an opportunity for women to get together and exhale in unison.

2) Perspective.

It's a real-world continuing education outside the classroom. Some have mastered how to deal with a difficult ex-husband or family member, others are on the far side of caring for older parents or grandparents. Our life experiences and skill sets are varied and valuable.

As a group, we have encountered many of life's most difficult challenges: death; divorce; family members with legal, medical, and mental problems; estrangements; financial setbacks; job loss; and other assorted heartbreaks. We've also experienced some sweet successes: lasting marriages and dating relationships; awards, promotions, and other career achievements; prospering businesses; exciting travel adventures; independent and thriving children; dramatic weight loss and healthy living—and our deepening friendships with one another.

Since learning paces vary and most of us have at least one "'A' for effort" life lesson we're still working on, we're a great wine-sipping resource of wisdom and alternate perspectives.

> *"I look around the table at all these women and see both 'where I was' and 'where I want to be.'"*
>
> -Cabernet Coach Kristin S.

3) Mirror of Better Self.

Some of us fight a tendency to play whack-a-mole with our self-diagnosed deficiencies—eyeing them, mallet in hand, intent on clobbering ourselves before anyone else can. *Thankfully, that's a "used to do it" behavior for me!* When a friend, through a little affirming conversation and commiseration, offers back a more generous reflection of you, that's powerful. We begin to see ourselves in a more flattering and, often, more realistic light. Of course, you aren't everything you want to be yet! Who is? But when you're in the company of others who can help you see your possibilities and the progress you have made, it's an invigorating nudge toward that better self.

Brenda, an exceptionally gifted portrait photographer, had pigeon-holed herself as a wannabe hobbyist. Her self-esteem had been eroded by a philandering husband. She saw herself as a devoted mom but defeated wife—*The End*—until a friend (me) recognized the remarkable talent displayed in Brenda's online photo albums. I begged her to take the cover photo for *Date Like a Grownup*, and she launched from there. While many of us can spot the "special" in one another, Brenda can evoke that inner beauty and then capture an image of that real ideal self. Not surprisingly, people love the images, even those who "never" take a good photo. *The only downside is the new challenge of scheduling lunch dates around her busy shoot schedule!*

> *"Whenever I have doubts and think, 'Am I good enough; can I really do this?' I remember what you said, how you called me out and insisted I have a gift."*
>
> -Cabernet Coach Brenda B.

4) Self Help Through an Other-Oriented Focus.

Our casual conversations can be excellent reinforcement of our own intentions. Often, the encouragement and gentle advice we give to a fellow friend is fresh from integration into our own daily life. *In the vein of the mom-to-kid, "I'm cold; go put on a sweater" thing but with a little more to back it up than a shiver.* I've overheard some pretty terrific advice shared between women navigating similar challenges, fortifying them both to "soldier on."

These weekly conversations certainly increase *my* fluency in many of the concepts I write and speak about. Occasionally, I have to pause to record or jot down wise words or a ridiculously funny story for later use.

> *"Ooh! Hold on a minute. That fits in with what I'm writing—need to save it on my phone."*
>
> -Cabernet Coach Heather D.

5) A Better Space-Filler Choice.

In Chapter Two, you read how Carol devoted herself to a career at the expense of emotional health and happiness. *Fear* of her pain automated her response to it. Her pervading loneliness triggered an overwhelming urge to work harder, longer, and better—because she could at least "win" at work. Ill-equipped to effectively deal with her husband's rejection, Carol recognized no other options for filling her lonely hours.

These days, she loads that once feared space with more thoughtful choices. Carol's calendar includes Sunday afternoon walks and road trips with friends. Her former friendless state would be *unimaginable* to anyone meeting her now! And this more balanced approach has only enhanced her career success as it helps fuel exciting new entrepreneurial ventures. She credits much of this life-changing connection to the relationships she has developed through Cabernet Coaches.

Similarly, many of the single women simply appreciate the choices created by a larger social network. A quiet night at home becomes a choice rather than the default Plan B in the absence of a man. Not surprisingly, this allows them to wait upon a higher caliber guy over the "least of the worst" dating options available at any given moment.

"Strong girlfriends reset me. Every time I get together with them, I feel at peace."

-Cabernet Coach Tessa T.

6) Red-Flag Finder.

We all need a few "you're kidding yourself" friends in our lives. You know, the ones who can listen to your rationale for the bad decision you're secretly *dying* to make and call you out on it. Oh, of course you can still decide to send a flaming email to your mother-in-law, fly off to visit the ex-boyfriend who is "just a friend," or sink money into a home upgrade that will vastly diminish your cash flow, but chances are you'll at least consider a couple of better alternatives.

And with mobile dating apps, it's easy, and often entertaining, for the single women to get occasional feedback on NowOrNever3 or SoloDad87...*"Ooh! He carried a man purse, and it was bigger than mine! Called it his 'kid bag,' but on a dinner date? Without any kids?!"* or *"He's a bit of a creep and spends an awful lot of time with his ex-wife if you know what I mean,"* or, even worse, *"That's my ex-husband."* Not all the news is good, but it's far better to spot those red flags before one gets planted in your heart.

"Only another girlfriend can tell you that after four days of silence he hasn't been too busy. Don't text him. Save your dignity."

-Cabernet Coach Kathy C.

7) Leaving Limbo.

A rut is fine if it's a precursor to a tree planting, but when it's simply the result of an indecisive rocking in place, the only thing you're going to grow is weary and repetitive. Limbo-living is the pause that depletes.

Whether due to a lack of confidence or knowledge, an unawareness of viable options, or an internal wrestling match, we're all at risk for the occasional blind spot. *"I'm so sick of this job." "I wish I were in better shape."* The default complaint often rolls loose without real brain engagement. But consistent connection allows friends to observe whether we're moving the marker or simply drawing deeper and deeper grooves in the dirt at our feet, and the Cabernet Coaches are good at providing inspiration and gentle nudges—valuable backup support—to help one another climb *out* of an unproductive rut. *"Your office environment sounds awful! Have you updated your resume yet?"* or *"Come to yoga class with me!"* or *"Don't wait on him to make weekend plans. Come with us to the Arts Festival on Saturday!"*

> *"I know it's the right choice, but it's hard! Don't think I could do it without you guys."*
>
> -Cabernet Coach Kayron C.

8) Ready Resource.

Whether one of the ladies is looking for a reliable plumber or a concert buddy, she's likely to find one through our ever-growing network of friends. We're Google, Yelp, and Trip Advisor in real time: with eye contact, far more expression, and the ability to grow just about anything into a fun shared experience.

Also, there's less pressure test-driving a new activity—*"Yoga class? Will there be any other beginners? Do I need to bring a mat?"*—when you know a friend has your back. Most of us are past the need for hand-holding, but there's a definite boost to the comfort-level knowing there will be a familiar face in an unfamiliar place.

> *"Now that my roof rack is on, my kayak is ready to swim! If anyone wants to go kayaking, let me know!"*
>
> -Cabernet Coach Janet D.

9) Social Skills.

We're reasonably skilled with the pithy texts and basic small talk essential to navigating daily life. But for those just emerging from a time of social hibernation, or an afternoon in a remote office cubicle, our weekly gatherings are a low-pressure refresher on how to develop more meaningful communication. Advancing past rote micro-conversations—"How are you?" "Great, and you?" "Good! And you?" *Oops*—into actual connection is great practice and a confidence builder for other less comfortable social situations.

It's fairly effortless to slide between one-on-one and larger group conversations with so many women within a table setting or two. Being amongst women who want you to shine, with however many lumens you have available on any given night, makes it easier to do so.

> *"I've never found it easy to be comfortable with people I don't know well, but everyone I've met through this group has made me feel welcome. I appreciate it more than you know."*
>
> -Cabernet Coach Theresa L.

10) Grows Hope.

It isn't a 'Misery loves company" thing but instead a "We're in this together" deal. Because we are. Actual support groups can sometimes develop into commiseration clubs with a lot of one-way leaning. They have their place, but don't necessarily foster the mutuality needed for healthy "grownup" friendships. Many of us have the contact information for appropriate and helpful groups that can provide focused support, but our Cabernet Coach gatherings are meant to be a sustaining and inspiring connection time. No one needs a lesson on how to wallow, but fellow travelers can be very helpful to our forward progress.

Many have echoed that "I thought I was the only one" feeling I lived with during and immediately following my divorce. Finding supportive social connection after a life-bending transition can feel like touching your feet to the bottom of a pool and finding the water isn't over your head after all.

> *"Just wanted to say thank you for listening last night. My emotions have been everywhere this past week. It helped immensely. So great to have girlfriends like you."*
>
> -Cabernet Coach Rose D.

OK! What's not to like, right? You're sold and want your ticket—Now! *Does it come with a commemorative cup?*

Connection Point

After you truly "face the space" and call it by name—*I feel lonely*...when you can admit that you aren't really too busy for friends, but that you simply don't know how to find them, you've removed an important barrier and can better respond to your psyche's warning message. *"Hey, this disconnected space feels really uncomfortable and unsafe!"* If you were hungry you would eat, if you were thirsty you might get a glass of water. But you're feeling lonely, so instead, you'll need to get connected.

I can't say this will be as easy to take care of as dry mouth or a delayed lunch, but it *will* get easier and life will get a lot better. One of my biggest thrills comes from the frequent comments of women in my Cabernet Coaches group—their personalized versions of "this has changed my life!" Connection does that for us!

I don't know your name or the circumstances that have brought you into this book with me, but if you feel even a *little* bit like I did, I'm really glad you're here. Disconnection *hurts.* I get it. So, this is personal. Me to you. And it's going to get better.

Connecting Thought:

I've lived like this long enough. It doesn't feel good, and this *isn't* how I want to live my life. No one else can change this for me. I have to be an active participant, but that's good, because it means *I'm* in charge of my actions and choices. And today, I choose to begin building the life I want to live in.

**Take a moment to imagine what this life could look like. What kinds of activities will you enjoy sharing with friends? Know that other women would also love to find someone like you with whom they could walk/talk/shop/dine/hike/travel!*

Someone else is hoping to find a friend like *me!* In fact, there are *many* somebodies around me right now just waiting and hoping for connection.

We often emerge from our original families with a faulty framework, and hanging anything on "crooked" is always a challenge.

Chapter Six

First Friends

When I first recognized and acknowledged *my* isolation, I had very vague ideas of what a good friendship might look like. Many of them grew from my early experiences with peer group females. My hope is that, while reading this chapter on early connection, you will tap into some of your own memories, both good and bad, and recognize their subtle influences upon your own picture of friendship.

> *"Wait a minute! There's another one!"*
>
> —Attending physician at the birth of my twin sisters, Stephanie and Suzanne

I have a framed photo of two-year-old me kneeling behind my sisters' double bassinet against a backdrop of prettily arranged Christmas packages. The proud announcement in the opposite side of the jointed frame announces the birth of "identical twin daughters." As a mom of three, I will forever be impressed at the very *existence* of this photo in which three sets of eyes are open, alert, and focused toward my dad's camera lens. I'm even smiling, although Mom once characterized that same expression as "bewildered." Viewing that photo from across fifty years, I now see that my hands are balled into tiny fists and that my smile might be attached to a toddler voice on the edge of a "Say Chee-eeze!" meltdown.

My parents aimed for textbook—more specifically, *Dr. Spock's Baby and Child Care*—sibling integration. They hyped my big sister status and gave me the master of ceremonies role for most of the "Are they identical?!" introductions. Three sisters within two years of age might have presented as an instant playgroup—I thought so too. But there was a whole lot of cute in that bassinet, and paired with some other challenging family dynamics, my sisters' births often felt more like the genesis of an exclusive, twins-only club to me. I adored them, but as they grew so did the circle of fans and friends around them. I was most often the sideline observer, left to admire—with a troubling twinge of envy—their easy access to a never-ending stream of neighborhood connections.

Truth be told, their own relationship had some limitations, as I found out after we had navigated our parents' and grandparents' deaths, a couple of divorces, and a general realignment of the family universe. *My* earliest views were based on envy of what looked to be an easier path. With a genetic match just across the floor of their shared bedroom, *my* presence had often felt extraneous—a mandatory accommodation. Strangely, older twin Stephanie's memories of those years sound very similar to my own, only she felt left out by me!

The more we learn, it seems the exception to grow up in a classically emotionally-functional home—*much to the benefit of contemporary culture as a crisis or two is essential to the development of any halfway interesting plot line. Or person.*

Nobody parents his or her children error-free, and most of us are well-served to make a few adjustments to our understanding of "normal" as we later merge with the world at large. But, that's seldom a priority as we busy ourselves launching toward adulthood, is it?

Not surprisingly, my three (with Kathleen) sisters and I exited childhood with some residuals that created drag in the years that followed. Despite our parents' best intentions, unresolved conflict, the competitive dynamics of five females living under one roof, and our underdeveloped communication skills fostered a subterranean current of instability and neediness.

Hello World!

A lot of what felt normal to me in terms of connection was, quite simply, a little off.

Such is the case for many of us: We emerge from our original families with a faulty framework, and hanging anything on "crooked" is always a challenge.

Your "normal" is relative, but your relatives aren't (necessarily) normal. Ba-dum ching.

I played the awkward social entrepreneur in those early years, making frequent attempts to ramp up my sisters' tepid enthusiasm for a third wheel via value-adds in exchange for inner-circle inclusion. In my efforts to secure a personal bestie, I demonstrated a precocious talent for marketing and promotion. Intuitively understanding the allure of the "exclusive," I proffered two-person book, movie, music, and travel clubs. Folded notes were carefully slid under their locked bedroom door—*Secret!! Private meeting for club officers in Heather's closet (on upper ledge) today at 3:30.* My business plan was simple and straightforward: Only one twin need apply. Guaranteed vice-presidency.

Résumé-building stuff for the lucky winner, right?

Divide and conquer.

"Trade Your Life Day" was another unique opportunity by which a twin would be given singular opportunity to be "the oldest," and per my promotional sell, enjoy all the perks that came with living in one's own room—affording *me* potential squatter's rights in her vacated bedroom space. I sold it well, including full use of my personal library and big sister clothes, but interest would wane when one of their neighborhood friends came to the door. It was hard to sell the concept outside of the family. *"Hi! I'm one of your twin friends today."*

Unbelievably pathetic, huh? But it happened; I was there. Most of my game plan grew out of the formulaic *Adventures of Nancy Drew.*[31] As my early heroine and ideal, Nancy had only to stumble onto a dilemma at the end of a first chapter for George and Bess—more groupies than friends—to whirl in as willing accomplices to the pursuit of Nancy's perfect life. The books never made clear how Nancy incentivized their participation. It seemed all she had to do was stand near her little mystery with a bucket of ideas, and friends would show up, paintbrushes in hand, for her Tom Sawyer "Let's find the ghost in the bell tower" adventures. Mysteries were minor in our suburb—*Mom: "Did the Hoyers get a new station wagon?"*—so I focused on process.

It seemed simple enough, but it wasn't. In my heart, I was a Nancy, ready to whirl us all into a world of companionable adventure. But again, and again, I found myself completely clueless on how to engage my chosen George and Bess as they played Barbies across the hallway. And my yearning desire to fit in, to be chosen and included, played out over and over through my childhood and beyond.

That longing—*you know what I'm talking about, right?*—comes from our developing relational self. Much of what we learn about the process and value of building connection comes from these early relationships.

Think back to your beginner best friends. That "best" was a big deal, wasn't it? It meant you belonged somewhere. For most of us, the class assignments in elementary school had less to do with the teacher, and everything to do with the friend potential we would find in the room. Finding a best friend established the ever-important question of who would sit by you at the lunchroom table and also provided a measure of personal joy in that structured world where happiness was a snow day and misery could move in with a teacher-inspired "opposites should attract" classroom project pairing. While teacher classroom assignment committees may have guided us toward our first friends, the "best" part was all our own. We chose them, and they chose us. Or didn't. Early friendships were often our introduction to heartbreak.

Loyalty was the prize. In the very early years, we gave our hearts freely. Completely. Best friends were "4 ever." Until they weren't. When "forever" reached an expiration date, it broke our hearts.

Unvarnished Disclosure: Best Friends Forever

An unrelenting downpour splashed the glass pane, making it difficult to see my target: the narrow space between two of the houses just beyond our swing set and backyard hedge on the opposite side of the neighborhood block. But stubbornly, stoically, I held my lookout, leaning heavily against the sliding patio door, tears dripping silently as I waited for heartbreak.

Colleen was moving out of my world.

She had been a daily part of my life for nearly a third of my six years. We had chased fireflies and her dog Fluffy, gathered nuts from the lawn beneath the shagbark hickory in her backyard, splashed in the sudden and serendipitous pools that appeared in the drainage ditch beside my house after heavy rains, and traveled to countless imaginary worlds—always confident in the knowledge that we each had a best friend in the other. Although placed in separate kindergarten classes, we loyally shared a bus seat beginning on that first day of school, drawing big girl bravery from our bond—*and the sight of our mothers trailing anxiously behind in a gold-paneled station wagon.*

I couldn't imagine life without her.

As my personal doomsday approached, Mom's assurances that life would go on and that I would find new friends meant little. As the oldest of three (soon to be four) sisters who had to share *everything,* Colleen was indisputably mine. Stephanie and Suzanne had a seemingly endless stream of playmates; *extra* friends even (and in fact, Colleen's move would make way for yet another). I had Colleen. And my best—*only* friend—had a new home waiting in Sturgis, Michigan.

Finally, the massive moving truck edged into view. While mom had explained that Colleen wouldn't actually ride in the back with her bike and bedroom furniture, I viewed the truck as a greedy predator that had swallowed my best plans for summer and the next school year. As it rumbled away, followed by the Post family's station wagon, my sobs burst free. I stayed at the window, reluctant to move, until it finally sunk in that there was nothing more to see. When Jill moved in and began playing with my sisters, I didn't like her. She wasn't Colleen.

Fortunately, when first grade began that fall, I was seated near the brilliant and beautiful Anne. Frankly, I was stunned to be her chosen friend. She was clearly so far advanced from the rest of us. If I could find a class picture from that year with Mrs. Payne at Wilson Hills Elementary, I'm sure I'd find a few exaggerations to my mental picture of an almost teenage willowy brunette, but Anne seemed more like an exotic visitor than fellow first grader. And she was kind.

When my beginner crush, Steve, wrote Anne's name on the lid of his pencil box, it made sense to me. I easily reconciled myself to aiming for the second-best test scores and spent many happy afterschool afternoons in her company, creating supplemental lessons for our classmates. *I know, Beginner Nerd 101.* Standing beside her as we presented Mrs. Payne with crossword puzzles of the week's vocabulary words for our classmates, I basked in the shared praise, completely aware that my contribution was more an eager obedience to "could you just color in all the little squares around the letters?" than any grand etymological idea. But I was OK with that. Anne liked me.

My mother seemed a little concerned at times. Anne was either an only child or the youngest in a family with older siblings. I remember her mom and dad seemed more like benevolent grandparents than PTA parent material to me. Their hands-free support gave Anne a lot of freedom and creative discovery time which seemed to work well for her educational and social development. As a five-year-old oldest child, I'd started first grade with little worldly knowledge. I lacked Anne's easy confidence, but frankly, I didn't yet know it was missing.

Mom and Mrs. Payne had a special conference later that year, and Mom shared the news as gently as she could. Anne and I were both smart, but Anne was at least second-grade smart and didn't really fit in our first-grade classroom. I cried.

When she was advanced midyear to the next grade (and possible one more beyond that—my memory is hazy), it again made sense, but she was soon gone from my life except for occasional awkward sightings as our lunch lines passed outside the cafeteria. Yes, I could now reasonably hope to get the best grades, and maybe even a shot at the debonair Steve, but I wanted a new "best friend" far more.

It turns out I had a gift for best-friending classmates who would soon move away; I repeated those forlorn goodbyes three more times in elementary school. My defensive, pragmatic response to this string of severed attachments was to begin viewing friendships as disposable—*big "oops" on that one.* Significant "private" family issues compounded my growing isolation, and I found it increasingly difficult to connect in a genuine way. Then one day, it was my own family filling up the moving boxes.

My family's big single move was a simple across-town upgrade to a custom-build with more bathrooms and a bigger water heater to keep pace with the growing mirror and shower demands of four pre-teen girls. But it was hard to switch schools in the middle of what my mom later admitted was a heavy-duty awkward stage for my inner butterfly-to-be. My parents tried to sell me on the increased opportunity to grow friendships at two middle schools—"You'll know everyone when you get to high school!"—but having a primary friend mattered far more to me than having a broad backfield.

Do any of these feelings resonate with you?

In high school, I finally found another true best friend in Laura. We met in a bathroom while hurriedly doing zit cover-up between classes. Sporting similar emotional wounds from our discordant families, we felt an immediate click, and

I finally downloaded years upon years of personal pain to a truly empathetic friend.

But I relied on her almost exclusively, and while we shared some common friends, that whole "gotta have a *best* friend" thing again proved unwise. When Laura opted to graduate a year early, Brenda found a boyfriend, and Kathy dumped me for a more popular group of girls, I was completely lost. "Where do I sit in the lunchroom?" lost. Ultimately, I solved my isolation issue with my first real boyfriend. Scott was a grade behind me and a little rough around the edges, but his family loved me, and he eagerly filled that immense space where Laura had been. Problem solved. Except for all those seniors-only activities, high school was covered. More or less.

My experiences are in no way remarkable. Rejection and heartbreak happen to *all* of us—they're basic features included with the standard childhood. *"Congratulations! You now own the two-parent middle-class model that comes fully equipped with siblings, a suburb, and regular church attendance. Looks like an automatic, but it's actually manual drive—go easy on the clutch when you shift gears. You get a few add-on features with your optional "Writer's package": super-panoramic windows, extra rearview mirrors, and enhanced GPS memory. Nice to have if you know how to use it, but it'll definitely impact your mileage if you don't. Check your pocket; the keys should be there. Enjoy driving your life!"*

Each one of us is a unique creation shaped by genetics and environment, continuously confronted with our own special mix of blessings and challenges. Here's the fascinating thing: Blessings can enhance or diminish us. Challenges can *also* diminish or enhance who we grow to be. It isn't what we're given, but how we respond and learn from these customizations to our journey that will determine the joy, or misery, of our lives.

Unvarnished Disclosure: A Moving Target

Kathy kept her expectations low. "Five elementary schools, two junior highs, and three high schools. Dad was in the military, so we moved about every three years."

"It took me years to realize that, while my childhood was a normal experience for a military family, it was in no way a 'normal' experience. It was sterile; I had no friendships that lasted more than two or three years. My only friends were the ones at *that* particular base or station. And I understood that when we eventually left, I'd have a few nice memories but would have to start it up all over again somewhere else."

The lifestyle impacted Kathy's development in many positive ways. "I got to see a lot of the world and became very adept at being the new kid." Her gregarious personality has served her well in careers as an entrepreneur, realtor, TV reporter, and radio talk show host.

But years later, in her fifties, Kathy became more aware of the deficiencies that the constant "load up, move on, no tears" military mode had left within her relational self. "I didn't develop friendships or traditions," and the age differences between the seven kids in her family left her with older brothers she could recognize on a street but would be hard-pressed to identify by personal description. "When people asked, 'Where are you from?' I never knew how to answer: 'Where I was born? Where I'd lived the longest? Where I'd just come from?'"

Facebook gifted her with glimpses of her childhood. "I have a horrible memory for people. No recollection at all. I think when you move so often, your mind can only hold so much. You deem them no longer necessary when they're gone. There was this guy friend I had at my third high school—he found me on Facebook. He remembered all these details about this hike we did with a group of friends, and I had absolutely no recollection of it at all."

In fact, as we talked, Kathy realized she could remember no childhood friendships, no friends prior to the high school from which she graduated.

"When I get friend requests, I usually click 'yes.' I figure we probably *were* friends at one time, but without Facebook, they'd all be nameless, faceless."

One college friend, however, was determined that Kathy remember her face. "Micah and I met at orientation—the only radio/TV majors in a room of one hundred freshmen, we developed a pretty deep bond."

Kathy had a fundamentalist Christian background, an embryonic sense of self, and no dating experience. Micah's history was more stable. Steady. "Micah dragged me out to my first bar, introduced me to "The Rocky Horror Picture Show," and taught me country-western dancing."

She integrated Kathy into college life and made herself an indispensable friend on multiple levels. "Micah told me I was pretty and let me borrow her clothes. She was very generous and self-sacrificing. I'd never had that before."

Her new friend was loyal. Encouraging. "She even typed my résumé when I applied for my first job at CBN (Christian Broadcasting Network)." Micah was two years ahead on her graduation path but accompanied Kathy to the family's base assignment in Albuquerque that summer and maintained contact after her graduation a year later.

When Kathy graduated however, she moved on and matter-of-factly closed the door. Or at least, she tried to. Contrary to Kathy's previous experiences, Micah refused to view their relationship as expendable and remained a persistent friend. Distance didn't diminish the fact of their connection. More difficult? Sure. Worth the trouble? To Micah, it was.

Before long however, their lives aligned again. Both women ended up working at CBN headquarters in Virginia where they enjoyed another deeply bonding experience that grew their history and cemented the friendship.

Ultimately, Micah's persistence broadened Kathy's understanding of friendship. Rather than a Point A to Point B experience, their friendship now spans a continuum that has included years of geographic distance.

Kathy gives Micah complete credit for their friendship.

"Micah was dogged. She wouldn't quit."

Unvarnished Disclosure: Undercover Family

Joanne laughed when I asked. "Oh boy. My family. My family was very, um...non-traditional, and I know that's shaped me immensely." She took me back to 1972, when her dad was a small-town police officer and her mom, a happy homemaker, blissfully raising eight-year old Joanne and her younger brother in a quiet New England community.

"Mom would have been happy living in our suburban colonial home forever, but Dad decided there wasn't enough excitement. 'I need to go somewhere with a high crime rate.' And my mom, who loved my dad, said, 'Well, OK, but you *do* remember we have two kids?"

"So, he researches what cities have more crime, and our options are Detroit, Los Angeles, and Fort Lauderdale. He took a pass on Detroit, decided L.A. was a bit far, and ended up uprooting us all to the bedroom community of Coconut Creek, Florida. Being an adrenaline junkie, he soon decided that being a beat cop wasn't enough. He wanted to go undercover. So, we were the family on the block where for seven years Dad was a long-haired biker, and then for another seven years, he worked vice, with a Trans Am, leisure suits, and gambling."

"He adopted different personas."

"Yes! And we couldn't tell the neighbors why Dad was so odd, or why we had bikers coming over—he'd entertain the informants at our house. I mean, I'm sure some wondered if Mom was even with the same guy!"

"When Dad was there, he was larger than life, but he lived in that undercover world. The family was his second life. Mom tried. She was basically a single mom who worked full-time and came home to fix dinner with us. Dad occasionally joined us for supper, but it was a crazy wild life."

"You had secrets."

"Oh yeah. We just kind of had to accept that we were the ones the neighbors would always be scratching their heads at. And I guess I was always prone to that sort of isolation. I had a couple of friends and spent some time at their homes. They had what I didn't, a 'normal' family."

"How much could you share?"

"I'd tell them Dad was working on a couple of projects for his 'office.' That it was *almost* like he was undercover, but he wasn't. I didn't get into any details as to what gang he was riding with or where he was going. It definitely shaped me. As a kid, I sensed the danger but didn't fully process it until years later." She paused. "I don't know how we kept ourselves safe and sane."

"Of course, there were casualties. There was constant stress when Dad was around. Mom was unhappy. You obviously can't sustain a marriage in that kind of life, and when I turned seventeen, I was hell bent on getting out of that house."

Connection Point

Whether your memories of early friendships and family are good, bad, or non-existent, those years comprise the finger-painted canvas of your present-day social relationships. Impressionable little you took in a lot of information, but you absorbed it all through the eyes and ears of a child and processed that social data in a brain that would not fully develop until your early to mid-twenties. *Yep, there's a good reason many college stories end with "I can't believe I did that!"* Just as early exposures to food and music shaped your adult preferences, your early experiences with social connection have most certainly impacted your feelings about friendship as well as your approach and receptivity to it.

There's no need to dwell in your teens or twenties again, but revisit them for a short moment to consider how early friendships might currently affect your openness toward potential women friends: Are you quick to say hello with a genuine smile? Or do you often feel uncomfortable and wait on others to greet you first? Do you easily make eye contact? How much do you worry whether someone will like you? Are there parts of you or your life that feel "unacceptable"? Do you replay conversations in your mind, looking for hints of dissatisfaction and potential future rejection? How often do you instantly like or dislike someone?

We'll discuss the components of healthy connection in the next section, but in the meantime, understand that your methods and manner of communication and connection developed out of experiences that are yours alone. Realize also that every individual you meet brings an approach to social interaction formed through their own unique set of experiences, conditions, personality traits, and genetic tendencies.

Our need for connection and friendship is universal. Our approach to filling that need can differ dramatically from one person to the next.

Connecting Thought:

I need to remember that while every person I meet shares my need for good friendship, connection looks a little different to each of us. I will focus on what

I give with my greetings over what I get in return. What looks like disinterest to me might actually be shyness, insecurity, or simple distraction, so it will be a lot easier if I stop guessing and simply acknowledge the people around me. My "hello" is a gift that says, "I see you" and "You matter." Some will be grateful for it, and others may not even notice me, but that's OK, because it is truly brave and good to be a giver of connection. All interactions begin somewhere—more and more friendly connections are going to start with me.

I'm also going to begin growing "hello"s into conversations. Each of us carries a unique—sometimes surprising—storyline, and there is something valuable to discover in everyone I meet. When I ask how someone is, I'm going to focus on making eye contact and truly listening to their response.

"It isn't so much about what or whom our friends are but more about how they make us feel."

Chapter Seven

Why We Love Them and Why We Leave Them

Ask a woman what she appreciates or looks for in a friend, and you'll probably hear some variation of the following: "Someone who's loyal, non-judgmental, and has time for me." But if it were truly that easy, we'd simply usher the persistent lawn service company representative to a seat at the kitchen table to discuss auto-renewing treatment plans over iced tea and turkey wraps. Clearly, there's a lot more to developing deep connection than ticking off a few key buzzwords.

Our friendships can look very different from the outside. Some are easy, obvious connections: the tennis-playing suburban moms who ride together on all the school field trips, the softball teammates who meet regularly to watch basketball in the off-season, or the book club buddies who work their way through the year's Oscar nominations at their local movie theater. Others seem more random to the casual observer. Vivacious human resources recruiter Janet seems an unlikely friend match to the more introverted Dawn, a loan originator and freelance caterer, but their bond is tight and enduring. Air Force vet Kris is nearly fifteen years younger than travel agent Janis, but they had an immediate click the moment they met, share professional sports team loyalties, and include one another at the tiptop of their personal "best friends" lists.

My friendship with Kristi looks very unlikely on paper. She's a lively, multi-talented design and training director with a BFA; I'm her mom's age with three young adult children and a completely different set of life experiences. However, we have fascinating conversations during our lengthy bike rides, and I consider her to be a dear and valued friend. Turns out, it isn't so much about what or whom our friends are but more about how they make us feel.

Most of my best friends would not readily sign up for the adrenaline-laced vacations I love: hiking, kayaking, or cycling through new-to-me places or wandering around foreign countries with totally inadequate language skills. And by contrast, I'm not much of a beach girl myself—sure, I love an island, but the water's edge shots of pretty toenails against sparkling blue water don't send me running for a beach umbrella. On ocean visits I'm much more likely to be running the shoreline; hiking up a lovely mountainous backdrop; or completely submerged in my pursuit of undersea critters, slathered in SPF-a-zillion sunscreen with a snorkel-masked face, completely out of the Instagram frame until hunger kicks in at dinnertime. Surprisingly though, we all come back from our trips with pretty much the same effect. We're refreshed and invigorated. While perhaps a little wistful for the fading fantasy we indulged, we are also energized and even inspired as we plunge back into the reality awaiting us.

While we package our renewal times in dissimilar wrappings, they serve the same important purpose: to help us feel like our best selves. This is also what good friendships do.

What We Like

If I were to list some random favorite memories, I'd include the births of my three children, music with my dad, trail time with my kids, last moments with my grandma, a river of clouds in the Sierra de las Nieves, swimming through a glowing bioluminescent bay, and some lively, laughter-filled dinners in my home. *I promised "random!"* Your ideal memories might include a special vacation or achievement, a tender moment with a loved one, or a career success. So, what do any of these have in common? Allow me to indulge in a psychosocial version of the "I bet I can guess what you're holding in your hand" card trick.

In our alternately chosen but equally cherished moments, we felt emotionally and physically safe. Yes, there may have been a nerve-wracking and/or grueling preceding buildup—*check both of those boxes on the childbirths and mountain ascents!*—but they only sweetened the "all is right in my world" moment that followed, right?

We felt valued and respected. The moms amongst us might question my linking respect to something one cannot achieve without undignified shrieking and baring of body parts to complete strangers, but in my case, I felt stronger for enduring the rigors of pregnancy and labor and valued for bringing forth a beautiful, "best ever!" human being. Similarly, in those moments spent holding my grandma's hand and caressing her cheek after her world had shrunk to the dimmed space between us, I savored her presence. Knowing my approaching grief to be a measure of love, I could smile through my tears, grateful for her life and honored to share its final moments with her.

Examine your own treasured memories. My guess would be that at least one other person lives in each one. You were a participant in some way, not just an observer. You Belonged. Part of the treasure in each memory is that you knew this person was glad you were there.

In any of your selected memories, I bet you also felt like *you*. Genuinely *you*. For one glorious moment, you forgot what was "wrong"—the Thanksgiving Dinner tug-of-war with your sister or that the only clean spot on your car is where you accidentally brushed against it the day before. Instead, you were fully tapped into that central place within, stripped (or at least vastly downsized) of the worries and self-consciousness that often intrude upon our appreciation of a present moment.

And you were happy. Our favorite moments are joyful, whether quiet contemplations, momentous celebrations, or somewhere soft and wonderful in the wide-ranging middle. We've reached a worthy goal, experienced a deep connection, or we've stepped closer toward whom we hope to be or the life we're working to create for ourselves and others. You could hardly contain the smile that would eventually make your happy little cheek muscles ache or the grateful tears that totally wrecked your eye makeup. It was real, authentic happiness.

All of this makes sense with a quick glance at Maslow's original Hierarchy of Needs.[32]

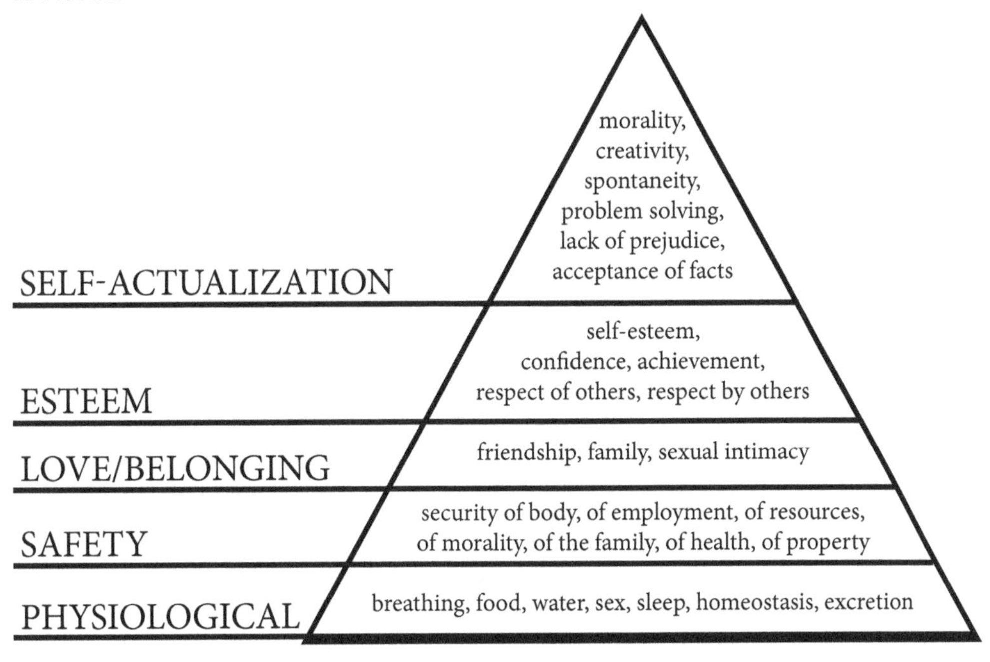

I'm working from the basic model for our purposes, but check out the illustration. It's standard Psych 101 but well worth remembering as an easy guide to our inner longings. Safety? Check. Love/belonging? Check. Esteem? Self-actualization? Double check. We want *all* of these—*as long as all those creature comforts at the physiological level have been duly attended to.* It makes perfect sense that we're more likely to seek out relationships that further our hopes of meeting these very important needs.

The Bridges

So what kinds of qualities spark the "Ooh, I wanna hang out with her!" reaction? While the women I interviewed shared uniquely personal experiences and sometimes chose a thesaurus "sibling" word to describe the appreciated quality, it's clear we fundamentally value many of the same traits when it comes to friends. We're more likely to work toward developing deeper connections with people who exhibit the following characteristics.

1) Non-judgmental

We are universal on this one. *None* of us wants to be measured against somebody else's standard of who we should be or what we should think or do. It's uncomfortable and completely unwarranted. Unless linked to the possibility of a promotion, academic degree, or prize, it's like rolling a garbage can to the end of your driveway and finding yourself swept, without warning, into a timed 10K. *But wait, I still have to grab the recyclables!*

A judgmental person is off-putting—maybe not immediately if you're one of the lucky ones initially given preferred status, but eventually, all those fine print qualifiers and restrictions will come into view, igniting either "What's wrong with me?" or "Who needs that?" depending on your own level of self-confidence. If allowed access, a critical personality may chip away at one's esteem, sense of belonging, and basic feelings of security. Few amongst us are motivated to chase after *those* feelings.

You may find some of my opinions and past choices to be illogical or ill-advised. *And I'm sure I'd agree with you on at least a couple.* So be it. Some of yours might be a bit surprising to me as well, but I'm OK with that. While expectations toward one's own self can be motivating, expectations aimed at other adults (excepting basic kindness and respect) are big, controlling boundary-breakers. A judgmental person is a self-designated CCO (Chief Compliance Officer) weighing and measuring those around them for their fit into the CCO's comfort zone, instead of allowing for grownup self-regulation.

Most of us have no difficulty judging ourselves. While the honest input of a kind and trusted friend can be valuable for detecting the blind spots that would impede us, this is an earned duty, and we tend to steer clear of the self-starters on this one.

Silent judgment is still heard, loud and clear, and judging others aloud is plain old gossip, a frequently cited barrier to friendship (coming up in the next segment). Judgment excludes. *Non*-judgmental people, on the other hand, are inclusive and accepting of another's ability to steer his or her own life. They may not agree, but they'll never try to wrench the wheel from your control.

Women are more drawn to the tolerant shoulder-shrugger than the demanding arm-crosser. Crossed arms say, "My way or the highway;" a shrug says, "To each her own."

2) Genuine

If I get a "You should have just *known,*" I'm likely to respond with "Why didn't you just *tell me*?"—not unkindly, but with genuine puzzlement. Please don't expect me to search out hidden meanings in spoken or written conversations. That would be an extreme overestimation of my abilities, and quite frankly, deciphering subtext is not my responsibility.

Many others feel the same. We get a little frustrated with people who constantly engage in one-way games of charades, because it's just too much work! There's a big difference between being tactful and simply burying your thoughts or feelings, expecting others to take on an emotional excavation project.

I know—sometimes we don't want to ask. We don't want to look vulnerable or to be a burden to others. We want people to *choose* to do the things that will make us happy, but we shouldn't have to *explain*. They should just *know*, right? *Anyone who agrees with those last two sentences gets a time-out!*

Expecting others who have had a *completely* different set of life experiences to think like us, to know or figure out how we feel, is ludicrous and, frankly, a bit self-centered. We're grownups, right? You say what you mean, and I'll do the same. Kindly, respectfully, and honestly. Women want straightforward friends; it's just easier that way. *Caveat! This must go hand in hand with another critical quality in our friendship-facilitating lineup: Kindness. Coming up shortly!*

Taking this a step further, real relationships require real revelation. "Imperfect" is quite OK with most of *us*. And if you think you made it this far without any errors, you haven't been paying attention. Being real means being relatable. Most of us can't identify with "flawless" and are a bit suspicious of the concept as a whole, apart from the carefully curated Instagram feed—*#Perfect!* Trying to bond with someone who won't share their true self is like pressing a refrigerator magnet to your forehead. It won't stick. Most flaws are not deal breakers; they're humanizing. We want to engage with fully-developed people, not one-dimensional facades.

Straightforward genuine people accept themselves. There are no chameleon-like personality changes as they move between social groups and situations because they're OK with who they are. Genuine friends make us feel more comfortable being who *we* are.

Kristin said it well in our interview. "If someone doesn't like your 'true self,' there are enough people in this world to let a few go." Amen.

3) Drama-free

"I don't have the time for that," and "Who has that kind of energy?!"

Drama used to be fun. You could even get academic credit for it. But most of us moved on to applauding children in school plays and grew less appreciative of live theater drama unfolding in our lives and relationships. While it took me a few years to self-extricate from those swirling sagas of inflated expectations and emotional wound-picking, once I did, I really liked how it streamlined my energy toward higher value pursuits.

At this point in life, many of us have come to terms with past co-dependencies and/or overactive nurturing tendencies. Managing our *own* emotions as we look for the grownup way to handle adult challenges and disappointments is demanding enough, so we avoid relationships that might trigger old, unhelpful behaviors.

Drama is *not* a string of difficult circumstances. Drama grows out of an individual's *response* to challenging situations and people. It escalates. It amplifies. "*I just know he's going to . . .*" "*But what if she . . .?*" Uncertainties portend future doom, and the broad spectrum of possibilities will be narrowed to the worst-case scenario. There is an obsessive engagement with the uncontrollable, such as other people or future events, and often, there is an avoidance of resolution in favor of anxiety and worry.

When women are *drawn* to fixing somebody else's drama, it may be an inadequate attempt to generate, as the "chosen" confidante or problem solver, those feelings of being valued and respected—of being needed—but it never works because the drama never ends. Instead, it swells into an energy sucking, time-filling, emotional dredging operation. The negative swings and mood volatility can tinge adjacent lives with a precarious quality, dragging a happy and productive afternoon into the play-by-play analysis of an unending power struggle. *So much for feeling safe!*

Also, pessimism can be contagious, potentially impacting even our base level need for rest if we begin losing precious sleep to anxiety or stress. The need is *never* about you or for you, personally. It's always about the needs of the lead character who may simply be looking for a willing audience.

It gets even trickier if, despite your best efforts, you become an unwitting target. We hate this, and many of the women I interviewed had a "never again" story. It's jarring to find one's self embroiled in sudden controversies, cast as a villain in ongoing drama with a friend whose feelings are easily hurt or who second guesses your motives. Initially, it can be difficult to disengage. "*She doesn't understand! I would never try to hurt her!*" You may feel compelled to fix it, to share your "truth." But sometimes, the drama perpetuator simply doesn't *want* to understand—because she's either addicted to the highs and lows of her own emotions or is getting mentally yanked back to past events that neither of you can control. Though difficult to conclude on such a painful note, disengagement is essential for the woman who aspires to fill higher level needs. Healthy people don't ride on someone else's emotional roller coaster.

4) Loyal

While instant "friend" clicks can and do happen, instant loyalty would feel a little stalker-ish to most of us. Legitimate loyalty requires a few hole punches on that friendship card to be proven real and valid. *"And you get a double punch for coming to Jenny's beginner violin concert!"* Blind loyalty is for the eternally optimistic sports fan. Friend loyalty grows in layers over time through quiet observations of character. That "all things being equal" favorable lean in your direction best emerges through seasons of friendship. It develops as we begin to see alignments with our other "must have" friend qualities.

Sometimes, we can get a sense of another person's ability to form loyalties in an initial encounter or conversation. Gossip and disrespectful attitudes will garner negative appraisal points and cause most women to proceed with caution if at all. We're looking for better things.

We instinctively trust some people. They remind us of someone we know or wish we knew. We perceive them as genuine and, thus, less likely to morph into some challenging competitive creature for whom we'll need to devise a quick exit plan. Our first assessments will be based on a lot of intangibles, including eye contact and body language, that will lead us toward, or away, from trust. The friend's friend who stands at her side but rolls eyes at what she says and criticizes her to others is the friend we don't want. There is no upside in potentially baring our souls to a sieve or exposing our vulnerabilities to someone who might later load them as ammo.

Milton Bradley's game of Life had reliable rules. When you stuck blue and pink pegs into your convertible car game piece—"Get Married!" "Congratulations! You have twin boys!"—they were yours to drive around with until game's end. Our real lives have remarkable amounts of fluctuation, so we ascribe great value to enduring relationships as a measure of our own stability. Ultimately, Trust multiplied by Time will reveal if you really have a Team vibe with someone. Does she want the best for you? Can she handle your flaws and forgive your mistakes? Can you each be genuinely happy for the other's successes, undiluted by twinges of envy? We want dependable friends and reliable relationships. A loyal friend makes us feel a little safer and happier in an unpredictable world. Loyalty affirms us.

5) Supportive

We want supportive friends, but (spoiler alert!) neediness, an upcoming barrier, can readily enable the dreaded one-way lean. How do friends provide support without creating an unhealthy and uncomfortable dependency?

Supportive friends will provide non-judgmental listening and encouragement aimed at enabling one another to tap into their own answers.

There are no "you should"s, and any "you could"s are tools of hope, offered without expectation.

Dependency, on the other hand, is more like a life preserver toss-and-tow to shore. There may be the hope that both parties will soon walk under their own power, but the relationship is based on the ability, energy, and commitment of one to carry and care for the other. This scenario evokes more of a medical/therapeutic or parent/child-dynamic than that of a true friend connection. Many difficult life events might require us to avail ourselves of such help for a time, but this type of bond, even under the *guise* of friendship, can't truly operate as one unless and until there is mutuality (coming up next) in the relationship.

Supportive helps. Dependency requires a carry.

Unvarnished Disclosure: Hoping for Hope

"It's been a different year," she reflected. "Friends that I've had for *years*—that I thought were *true friends*—it turns out, with a bump in the road . . ." *Wry smile.* "I lost a lot of connections. Some of that was just a natural drifting apart, but you realize a lot of it has to do with changing feelings. And life circumstances."

"You've had some big things," I commented.

Kristin and I had met in a support group for families trapped in the terrifying grip of anorexia and other eating disorders. Not a place any mother ever wants to be, and yet there we sat, rigidly perched on the edge of our seats, clutching tissues and just barely containing our anguish. The facilitator, whose son had recovered many years before, opened the meeting, and awkwardly, our circle of strangers began sharing deeply personal stories of guilt, shame, despair, anger, and terrific fear.

Kristin remembered. "So, I'm looking around this circle of intense pain, hearing increasingly scary levels of horror, trying to process what I'm hearing in my very first support group meeting."

I nodded. While our daughters had both been through frightening hospitalizations,* we listened that day to what could come next: permanent health issues, lengthy and costly out-of-state treatments, foreclosures and bankruptcies, collateral damage to siblings, and irrevocably fractured families. And, of course, death. You wondered how some would manage to rise from their plastic chair at meeting's end.

"The next speaker was an opposite," Kristin added. "Picture perfect. 'Everything's *great.* Daughter recovered and doing well.' I sat in that chair, committed—because I couldn't exactly leave—thinking, 'I can't handle listening to this!'"

"And then I hear someone saying this is hard and horrible, but that there's hope. It was you. We were dealing with a lot of the same awful mother/daughter issues, and you were saying, 'I don't want to carry that anymore.' There was love and pain; it was all real."

She connected.

"I've always been prone to isolation," she admitted, "but Parker's illness, the pain of it, was life altering from a parent's point of view. Eight years of guilt, of the questions 'What am I doing wrong?' and 'OMG, how do I help someone in denial?' Then there's just survival, and 'I can't live like this,' and then back to guilt. Pain. Fear. It's funny, you go through life thinking that you're independent and doing all these things and crossing them off your checklist. Then something happens, and you find yourself wondering, "Who is there to help me through this?" Feeling *so* alone. I felt like I was on an island, asking, 'Who are my friends?'"

"People would ask me, 'How are you doing?' And I'd think, '*Do you really want to know?'* They didn't."

"I'd been asking my husband for months, 'How do I find friends?' His joke was always to go on Craigslist. 'You'll find *lots* of friends on Craigslist.' But when we (she and I) walked out of that support meeting, we had a definite click. It was in speed dating form. We had *so* many commonalities; I could see myself in you. It was instant. Kind of 'Here it is, a good fit. Talk!'"

I nodded. Smiled. Kristin is simply a really cool person. *You'd love her too!*

"There was a lot of hopelessness in that room. I think we both wanted to hope."

There's full on "support," and then there's "supportive." The first builds, feeds, and stokes the fire; the second gently fans the flame. Kristin and I returned to the support group one more time and left feeling that a supportive friendship might be more useful to us both. In the months that followed we listened, we encouraged, and together, we hoped. Recovery from an eating disorder can be slow, and regaining peace of mind for the mothers, forever in love with their darling daughters, can be even slower. But it came for one and then finally, the other.

When Kristin and I update one another on our daughters, we listen carefully, and we fully appreciate. We share their successes with a poignant sort of joy, as loyal fans who will forever savor their victories.

*Happily, both our daughters have made full recoveries and grown into smart, beautiful, healthy young women. I like to tell people that Hannah is who I want to be when I grow up. *Smile.*

6) Mutuality

Our friendships are purely voluntary. These most personal investments come with no contracts, vows, or formulaic reward systems, and they best develop from a level surface with both parties contributing to the endeavor. There is an expectation of continuous reciprocity and cooperation.

When a friendship is evenly weighted, there's a gentle rhythm to this give-and-take exchange of time and energy. It isn't transactional, but there's a sense that *both* parties believe the relationship to be a worthy investment. You're never out of touch for long because there's an instinctive reach by *both* of you toward connection. You try to remember one another's details—to ask about an important meeting, an ailing parent, or if the blind date gets a "thumbs up" or immediate deletion. Either of you might suggest a Saturday bike ride or a Sunday brunch, and a "not this time" doesn't feel like a devaluation, it's simply an answer to a single, specific question. Quite simply, you both feel important to the other.

All relationships, friendships included, require a bit of work, but mutual relationships don't *feel* like work because there's fair compensation; *each* of you reaps the rewards of an authentic, supportive connection. While there can be an ebb and flow to the exchange, if the tilt is *always* or *mostly* to one side, it's a one-way relationship. Most of us will pick up on that vibe instinctively and step back. The friendship fade-out begins when we simply quit giving. We tend to be less interested in people who are less interested in us.

7) Prioritization

Mutuality's cousin might be prioritization. They're related, for sure, but live in differing contexts and were identified as separate characteristics by the women I interviewed. Mutuality has to do with shared levels of appreciation and cooperation. Over time, a mutual appreciation and a few shared interests can grow into a pretty solid friendship. Or not. Prioritization will impact how a relationship lives—or dies—within the greater, sometimes unwieldy world.

Most of us keep running to-do lists that orbit in brain space until we find them a parking space on paper, digitally, or maybe, in shout-outs to a proximate human. *"Mom, you don't really expect me to remember that, do you?" "Of course not, honey. Never mind." Gotta stop doing that.* Other than handwritten grocery lists, my tasks are now recorded as digital calendar entries that can be edited—bumped ahead—when I inevitably run out of time. There's less stress when I can view my own limitations as adjustable. Moving less critical items to another date or time ensures they aren't forgotten, but neither do they impinge upon greater priorities.

I have to admit, however, that a few of my "should"s bear virtual bruises from all the bumps they've endured. For instance, "Work on Christmas Photo Albums!" seemed an immediate "must do" when I optimistically anticipated a late-October window. Now, with a college FAFSA form to complete, chapter deadlines to meet, and some upcoming interviews and events to prepare for, those photo albums have been nudged—day by day by day—into late-November, with the bottom-line deadline now typed in boldface: *FOR REAL!!!* The albums, long overdue, *are* important. I hope to regularly gift my kids with memories of our adventures since they don't have the easy family photo access I enjoy, but they are a postponed priority in light of time-critical calendar interlopers. We all do this, right? It's basic personal life management.

When we bump a relationship however, we're more or less reassigning it with a virtual deli-style ticket number. "Sure! I'd love to get together. Um... but not this week. Or next. It's such a busy time right now! Tell you what, let's check our calendars and set something up for next month, maybe?" *Now serving number 47! Sorry ma'am, there are several people ahead of you.*

Just as "She makes time for me" will grow a friendship, a free floating "Soon!" without a tether to actual time and place will let one get away. Not to suggest that friends should expect to leapfrog one another's other commitments and responsibilities, but our choices most definitely reflect our priorities, chosen or assumed.

Top priority? Nah, that would be a little needy, now, wouldn't it? But to count you a friend, we expect to find ourselves on the list, well above random strangers and vague ongoing busyness. *Number 47? 47 . . .? Now serving number 48!*

8) Sense of Humor

It's no surprise that we're drawn to humor over drama. Smiles are automatic mood elevators and far better for our health. Complex plot lines create stress. Stress and worry impact physical health and brain function *and* will leave an illustrated map of the emotional journey across your forehead. Laughter, on the other hand, is the valve that *releases* mental toxicity. Our bodies can't even differentiate between a polite titter and the real thing (which is the science behind Laughter Yoga)![33] Not to suggest humor at the expense of authenticity—blithely skating over dilemmas and doom—but we are the sum of our many choices. *Apple or chips? Act or procrastinate? Wobble on or wallow?* With a good laugh, we breathe more deeply. Somehow the air seems cleaner and more worth the inhale.

Having a sense of humor doesn't require the quick-witted skills of a stand-up comedian, which is good news for those of us who habitually butcher the punch lines. "*Wait a minute, I should have said...um, let me just start over.*" What we're actually looking for is an *ability* to laugh—at one's self and at the occasionally ridiculous twists and turns of life. It's a chosen perspective that helps us launch off of those mountains and molehills that, should we crash-land, could easily jangle our brains and bruise our hearts. While we appreciate empathy and sympathy, we value even more the one who can help us find hope. Humor helps diffuse concentrated worry and allows the first rays of the broader perspective to poke through a gloomy outlook.

Cancer, autism, cystic fibrosis, and single parenthood—this list doesn't sound like the laugh track for a life, does it? And yet, to hear Nikki recount the ups and downs of parenting a special needs child and a "love you today, hate you tomorrow" teen-aged daughter, all while working as a self-employed hair stylist who *occasionally* tries to dip a toe back into the dating pool...When she shares the many challenges of her life, there is usually a punch line. Obviously, none of these issues are amusing, but thankfully, Nikki learned long ago how to find joy and laughter regardless of how easy or difficult life is on any given day.

We first met in her hair studio; me, merely hoping to find a new stylist within a short drive of my house who could handle my curls, and she, ready to work her magic on a 10:30 AM new client appointment. I can't remember what prompted the first laugh, but it rolled steadily back and forth between us at that first meeting, cementing an undeniable friend "click."

She's weathered some significant challenges, constantly rescheduling life and work around the medical needs of her sweetly quirky, Spiderman-worshipping son Jackson, while simultaneously balancing against the very different needs of "Mom, did you really just say that?" daughter Taylor. Nikki has embraced it all because the alternative at the hardest times might be to stand around with empty hands, and "grateful" simply feels better.

Sure, it will be fantastic if the newly approved medication is effective in reducing Jackson's cystic fibrosis symptoms. And a recent cancer diagnosis has left Nikki short one kidney and facing a career adjustment as the cancer appears to be linked to workplace chemicals. She has a few things to figure out as her body heals.

But she's so happy to be alive! Quite typically, she found humor within all the medical tests and hospitalizations, even reminding her surgeon to be mindful of her "still single" status as he marked incision lines. Over lunch last week, she could even give a half-laugh over the almost-boyfriend (they'd been dating three months) who unceremoniously met her parents by walking into general family hysteria over her diagnosis and then disappeared for about three weeks, only to text, more or less, "it's not the cancer, it's me."

"Right." Nikki rolled her eyes. "He text-dumped me!" But she laughed, realizing the cancer saved her some time. After losing a kidney, the loss of a socially-inept guy feels more like a good haircut.

Atypically, Nikki made me cry the other day with a voicemail message that I've locked and saved. About our connection. Our friendship. "We manage to have fun and still talk about these things that no one really wants to talk about." There was a lot more. Nikki's words made me think about how our shared laughter and humor immediately swept the landscape free of polite pretense and left us space to be comfortably real.

"Sense of humor."

"Can't be so serious all the time!"

"Need to laugh."

We all do—science says so. In a world filled with real-time daily docudramas, we seek the good medicine of a light heart in potential friends.

9) Fluent Kindness

We teach it to our children and search for it in prospective romantic partners. Not surprisingly, women also prize kindness in potential friends because it generates all the wonderful kinds of feelings we crave as we're growing into the upper levels of our "best self" pyramids.

Kindness comes in many forms. Sometimes it's active—"Please, I insist; that's for *you*!" But at other times, kindness is evidenced by an individual's restraint: a removal of self from a situation. Kindness might be alerting someone to a shorter event admission line while refraining from mentioning the half-price ticket you scored—*Yes!* —for the same event.

While a singular act of apparent kindness may draw notice, a pattern of thoughtfulness will draw friends. Not only do considerate people make us feel more safe, secure, and worthwhile, they often pull our own intentions up a notch or two, helping us to be a better version of ourselves. This kindness contagion has a two-fold benefit: Behaving generously feels good because it affirms that we are in a position to *be* benevolent, *and* we've simultaneously exposed something beautiful from within ourselves. It can be an upgrade to our self-identity.

Politeness and tact are simple essential marks of civility. With reasonable amounts of self-respect and confidence, we expect them. Kindness is different because it is so variable. If Politeness were a "Congratulations," "Best Wishes," or "Get Well" greeting, specially chosen for a notable occasion or condition, Kindness might dwell in the "Just Because" or "Thinking of You" row of blank cards sitting alongside, undefined and awaiting random selection. We value it highly because its appearance, while always welcomed, is often a surprise.

It doesn't even need to be aimed in our direction. Good sportsmanship, non-parentally mandated sharing by a child, generous words from one political opponent to another—*use your imagination here...*These things make our hearts swell with a bit of hope, so we love to spot kindness in others.

While single acts and responses may, of course, cloak ulterior motives, *fluent* kindness—a prevailing attitude of thoughtfulness toward others—reveals a chosen lifestyle. It's a click-through photo gallery peek into where someone lives.

What might fluent kindness disclose about a potential friend? Maturity, because a kind person can rise above pettiness. Generosity of spirit, because a kind person seeks to make the world a warmer place simply because they can. "Other awareness," because a kind person is giving something of value by word or deed rather than working only to build their own little kingdom.

These are qualities that nurture the best in us. We want to be near these people because these are the people we want to grow to be.

Unvarnished Disclosure: You Needed It

"Something would happen. He'd say something or there would be some behavior that confused me, and I'd think, '*Where did that come from? I didn't grow up this way!*'"

The marriage therapist privately confirmed to Anna that her husband had some mental issues. "I was so relieved! She said, 'You aren't the root of this problem.'" But Anna was entangled in a very real and disturbing problem nonetheless.

She eventually decided to end the marriage, but Dan's desperate reliance on her manifested in extreme anxiety whenever Anna even broached the topic of separation. Time and again, she would start strong only to quietly back away, unwilling to push through the emotional turmoil. It grew into the worst kind of limbo-living. Anna kept the peace but lost more and more peace of mind as she structured her life around enabling Dan's stability. "I was working seventy-four hours a week. Traveling a lot. Exhausted." Not surprisingly, the stress generated a depressive state. When she finally set aside her laptop and pulled up the bedcovers at night, she would lay awake in the dark for hours, her mind spinning through a jumble of thoughts and worries.

I had asked her about a friend's kindness to her, and Anna teared up at the memory. "It was then, when I was going through all of that with Dan. So miserable...I went over to her house one night."

"It's funny; she was really a friend's friend back in high school, but we just clicked. We claimed one another as sisters because our own sisters were—" Anna made a face.

"So, I showed up at her house, and we talked. I just kind of spilled things. Everything. And then she insisted—because I was so exhausted!—on my getting some rest. She took me to her room, had me lie down in her lovely, cushy, wonderful bed, and closed the door.

"When I woke up, it was afternoon of the *next day*! I'd slept almost twenty-four hours! I was a little embarrassed, and said, 'Why didn't you just wake me up?' I mean I was sleeping in *her* bed! And she just said, 'You needed it.' That was it. 'You needed it.'"

She grabbed a napkin off the kitchen counter. "It was *so* kind—still makes me cry!"

The Barriers

These are the walls we unwittingly build around ourselves, and they can be a difficult tear-down project; because while it's pretty easy to identify these behaviors in others, we tend to wrap them up in semi-plausible excuses when it comes to ourselves.

Often, these barriers are simply bad emotional reflexes—ineffective default responses that communicate completely different messages than intended. *Nobody* muses, *I really want to work on my pettiness* or thinks, *I could really be a lot better at disrespecting others.* Nope, these traits will never make a New Year's Resolution list for self-improvement! But these behaviors can easily creep into our interactions. We don't choose them so much as they attach themselves to us, like goo on a shoe, when we're feeling less than the happy confident selves we aim to be. I won't belabor them, but we do need to note them—because women definitely notice them. We don't want to see them in ourselves, and we usually avoid building close friendships with women who host these types of unwelcome behaviors on a regular basis. We choose friends who will be supportive of our gradual ascent up Maslow's Pyramid and steer clear of those who might throw an elbow.

1) Gossip and Pettiness

The underlying intent is often a "here I am, notice me" sort of nudge, but it's a poorly executed effort at connection that quickly declines into a dine-and-dash consumption of embarrassing details and ugly innuendo. This word feast is the wrong sort of hospitality, a shared meal absent any uplifting fellowship. The hope is often to display or obtain an insider's knowledge or to fix a perceived slight to self. "When we were neighbors, she used to . . ." or "I heard he has an issue with . . ." The actual message, however, is *completely* different: *"I feel better about myself when I can prove that I'm superior to someone else with any means available to me."* Or maybe, *"I want you to like me, so, here! Allow me to give you some super private information so that you can appreciate how connected and smart I am!"*

A similarly insecure individual may draw a temporary sense of belonging from this, but at some level they realize their own vulnerability to the speaker's insecurities. The listener will correctly perceive self-doubt and instability—and realize that anything she discloses can and will be used against her should there be an opportunity to do a social pull-up on the information.

2) Selfie Mode

"I kept trying to change the channel, but she always flipped the conversation back to herself! Every time!"

Sorry ladies. Unless listeners have paid Ticketmaster a processing fee for the honor of hearing the discourse on your kid, job, vacation, ex-husband, or gluten-free diet, this is *anti*-Dale Carnegie stuff! *How to Thin Friends and Irritate People* comes to mind. Despite the pervading presence of celebrity Instagrammers and YouTubers, *none* of us is so fascinating as to merit monologue conversations.

Now, an excess of "me talk" can easily spring from nervousness or a lack of confidence; I get that. Most of us can understand and sadly relate to a cringe-worthy moment or two in our past. *Me to Me: OK. You can stop now. Really...time's up! Stop talking, Heather. I mean it!*

And then there's the "stuck in crisis" mode, be it fear, regret, or anger. At this point in life, we've all been through some heartbreaks and challenges and understand how these can overwhelm thoughts and conversations. But a spin cycle, where every updraft is quickly yanked back down, will soon dizzy even a committed friend. We're game for leaning in with a supportive shoulder to help one another gain traction out of a rut, but if the desperate desire to find a boyfriend or angst over ancient history *always* wins, the potential friendship loses. There are highly trained professionals who are actually paid for that sort of work.

And then there's good old-fashioned narcissism. The narcissist truly believes it's all about them. You cannot lead them onto other paths, because they live in Rome, and all roads circle back. There's a lot of talk about narcissism; social media and politics provide myriad opportunities for us to indulge in a bit of amateur psychoanalysis, but the truth is that we all have degrees of self-centric thinking. *Never* thinking about yourself can be just as harmful. But yes, most of us are aiming for the tippy top of the pyramid where we can readily appreciate the value of *all* life journeys. The narcissist is simply playing King of the Hill.

It's impossible to build a genuine mutual friendship with a true narcissist. Dysfunctional dating and marital relationships sadly happen all the time, but friendships? Not so much. It's just not that fun.

And hey, if you're worried that *you* might be a narcissist? Congrats—you passed! Entertaining that thought makes it more likely you aren't one at all but suggests you may have spent a bit of time trying to disengage from one[34]—*and probably have **no** desire to try developing a one-sided friendship with another one!*

3) Negativity

Well, of course! Had you sat with me for an interview, I bet you'd have told me the same thing, right? Negativity is so, well, negative! None of us want to be around that. And none of us want to be that woman.

But here's how we sometimes trip over our own standard: "Well yeah, that's true, but I want to be *realistic.*" Somehow, we convince ourselves that to be realistic, we need to prepare for the worst. *Ten percent chance of rain? Cancel the picnic!*

"But I don't want to get my hopes up."

Valid point. And as I'm writing this book, it would be foolish and completely *un*realistic to send off "save the date" cards to celebrate its future bestseller status. But if I were to instead swing back in the opposite direction—*No one will ever read this if it even gets published*—this would be my final sentence.

(Dramatic pause)

Right back there. In the previous paragraph.

So, while it's unwise to count on the best possible outcome, expecting the worst is kind of overkill, don't you think? It's like driving through life with your parking brake on, annoying all the drivers behind you. Realistically (indulge me), to be "realistic" means to aim high, but to carry a general expectation (for planning purposes only) of landing in the wide-ranging middle while actively focusing on what is actually within your control: your own efforts. Worrying about all the bad things that could possibly happen—*"If we can't fix this, there goes my career"*—is a pretty significant waste of energy for you and everyone else in earshot.

Which is why all of us eventually back away from negative people. *"Well, nice talking with you. I hope something works out!"*

4) Competitiveness and Disloyalty

Competitiveness is like the accidental whispering of private information near a live microphone. *"I want to belong!" "I need to feel more respected!"* Only somehow, the speaker never hears the message she's inadvertently broadcasting. So, she tends to do it again and again, proclaiming her insecurity and isolating herself more and more.

It can be both a cover-up and a desperate grab for the imaginary rung on a ladder she climbs alone. The goals? A sense of belonging. A stronger self-esteem. Unfortunately, this method of nudging herself ahead by pushing others aside, with frequent sideways glances to assess her progress, virtually assures her failure. We can't form a true bond with someone intent on using it as an elastic band from which to launch up and beyond us. And she won't find affirmation in alienation.

Yes, we've all felt those little surges of jealousy somewhere along the way. Maybe you and a college friend shared mutual interest in the same oblivious guy. Or perhaps you couldn't help noticing how much easier things seemed to go for a female colleague—*"Well, team, once again Jackie came through for us!*" As developing women, it was hard *not* to compare. We'd been graded on Bell curves, competed in sports, auditioned for plays and choral groups, and vied for first jobs and promotions. It's understandable that we might have occasionally extended our areas of legitimate competition off the field. Embarking on our journeys, most of us quietly questioned our ability to read the map and wondered if we'd even chosen the right destination. We looked for feedback and reassurances. Hopefully, over time, we grew confident in self-navigating and learned it's OK to detour and ask directions—because it is and we can. And ideally, we grew happy enough with ourselves that we can be genuinely happy for others.

But some women still wonder and worry: "*Am I ahead yet? Am I good enough? Do they like me?*"

Competitiveness will manifest in name-dropping, one-upmanship, and "me" talk. There may be little jabs, as if a little poke to *your* esteem will somehow inflate *hers*. The drive to fill those psychological needs of belonging and self-esteem is strong, and if channeled into social competitiveness, will generate a jarring vibe, an undercurrent that puts other women on guard. Depending on how far others have journeyed in their own quest for belonging and esteem, when confronted with such behavior, they'll either respond in kind or carefully maintain a safe emotional distance. Either way, it's a disconnect.

Almost every woman I interviewed cited competitiveness as a friendship killer. We can't forge a trusting relationship with someone silently cheering for our failure as a measure for her own relative success.

5) Disrespect

It can show up in frequent last-minute cancellations and habitual interrupting. There may be a disdainful attitude or a disregard for personal property, feelings, or another's time. Disrespect is an underlying attitude that can pop out in a number of ways, but it all feels like a linebacker-sized cold shoulder.

Women described acquaintances who were always late or who treated them differently in social settings. "She ignored me!" Or there was casual use of personal property. "She never asked." Forgotten promises that led to hurt feelings. "She said she wanted to celebrate my birthday, and then I never heard from her." It wasn't a singular occurrence but a pattern of inadvertent carelessness that sent a clear message: You don't matter as much as me.

Obviously, this doesn't do much for the woman trying to grow a healthy love for herself. Disrespect is a pickaxe to our progress, and women avoid building friendships with sisters likely to tear down or put a chink in what they're trying to build.

6) Possessiveness

You know the one...the friend who doesn't want you to have other friends. *Shiver. Cringe.* It's uncomfortable. Suffocating. She expects immediate responses to her frequent texts and phone calls. Your independent activities stir up waves of hurt, and she is intent on proving her BFF status.

This is grade school stuff. Clinginess—neediness—generally indicates that a woman has a big space in her life and is intent on stuffing it full with *your* life instead of building her own.

It's exciting to find a friend you click with, and sometimes you're lucky enough to meet one who shares your sense of humor, favored activities, and food preferences. You hang out a lot because you're often headed in the same direction and it's more fun going together. There's an intimacy that can feel similar to a romantic relationship. However, the friendship stands a far better chance of enduring if both parties keep paddling their own canoes.

Unvarnished Disclosure: Too Much

"There's definitely a learning curve," she said, remembering the years immediately following her divorce.

"When we were married, there were 'work friends' and 'couple friends,' but we didn't really know each other as individuals. The women and I never grew close. I guess we (Rosalyn and her husband) were more of a friend 'unit.'

"After we split up I realized, 'I need to find *my* life.' So, I did the networking groups and met new people; there was a trickle down. You seek; you find. But, you also find people you don't *want* to find! I'm getting a lot better at being acquaintances first and not jumping in too quickly."

We were talking about bad friendships, and Rosalyn immediately remembered an early friend who had attached far too quickly. They were at the same point in life and had some things in common. Rosalyn was grateful for new friendships.

"But she got so demanding! You know, 'You didn't return my calls!' The woman wanted to hang out every weekend. It was too much.

"The kicker was, there were two times when I saw her and thought, *Huh! I have those same earrings!* But I didn't. I mean, I went home and found I didn't have those earrings anymore! And there were these two really cool glasses, Lily Pilsner stemware I'd found at T.J. Maxx. Gone. Then, a nice polo shirt came up missing; I see her a couple of weeks later, and she has it on!" She shook her head with a laugh.

"How did she—"

"Oh, you know, she'd stay over sometimes. We spent *so* much time together. And there were always things coming up missing. My nice shampoos, my splurges would just disappear, and I'd wonder, *Who would have taken that?*"

Possessive? I'll raise you to disrespect and property theft!

"So, did you try and talk to her about any of this?"

Rosalyn was silent.

"Or just let it die?"

"I let it die. The friendship. It was just—" She shrugged her shoulders.

Too much.

7) Neediness

While possessiveness can be demanding, neediness pesters the conscience. It tweaks pity, sense of duty, and our caregiving tendencies. It can feel like a constant call to be the human guardrail along a steep cliff, and spending time with this person can stir up anxiety and twinges of guilt. "What if I don't . . .?" But at some point, you realize the continual rescues are impacting you and your own nearest and dearest. You've been conscripted into somebody else's battle against their own self.

Emotionally healthy women will flee from a needy man. When it comes to needy women, we tend to back away slowly, proffering meager excuses until there's enough distance for a quick wave and dash to safety. We don't want to hurt their feelings. They seem so fragile!

But do we want to hang out with them?

Politely, but decidedly, "No."

They may have difficulty making decisions—*"What should I say?"*—or poke at you like a piñata, in hopes of releasing compliments and affirmations. *"I guess nobody liked my chili; there's half a pot left."* *"I'm too fat/skinny/tall/short/old/ugly/boring."* We may truly want to help and may do so for a while, but the relationship feels more charitable than friendly. We'll readily share a therapist's number or our favorite website for inspirational quotes, but neediness can feel like a continual "ask"—for time, attention, and affirmation. A constant prodding to fill someone else's emotional tip jar quickly strips any overlay of mutuality from the relationship.

It's more of an unpaid internship than a friendship, and while most of us can sympathize, we'd rather pour energy into any established relationships we have than take on a new project.

***

Here's the kicker. Most of these barriers—gossip and pettiness, self-absorption, negativity, competitiveness and disloyalty, disrespect, possessiveness, and neediness grow out of loneliness. Yes, the very thing we're trying to *quell* in our lives can, and does, actively *grow* these barriers that isolate us, *and* we're wary of other women exhibiting these unattractive behaviors—women who likely feel very much like *we* do on the inside.

Barriers are often the defense we heave up when we don't know what else to do, like the direct dial dinner default you call for carryout or the nondescript sweater you throw on when there's no time to poke around in your closet. These barriers are a pre-patterned response to fear and anxiety, and when we're lonely, fear and anxiety greet us at the door of almost every social situation. *"Heather, great to see you again! Take a look at all these people! Btw, I think you're a bit overdressed, and I'm pretty sure everyone in this room is far more interesting than you. Go get 'em! Oh, and try not to spill your coffee like you did the last time."*

So, what do we do with all that? We *want* to build bridges and find new friendships, but at the same time, those of us who most long for connection may be unwittingly blockading access to it and, understandably, avoiding other lonely women who are doing the same thing!

Sometimes we just need to throw out some orange barrels and do a little reconstruction. That urge to share a bit of gossip will be transformed with the growth of bridges like a non-judgmental attitude, kindness, and bonds of loyalty where merited. And to reduce an anxious focus on yourself, concentrate instead on reciprocity (building mutuality) and prioritizing others in your life. *And a sense of humor always helps!* Humor is also a great replacement for a negative perspective—if you can find a laugh, you can find a way through. An active focus on being supportive and facilitating give-and-take mutuality can help temper possessive urges. Integrating kindness, supportiveness, and loyalty will better communicate respect. Building mutuality, prioritizing others, and developing a better sense of humor can help us quell feelings of neediness. And getting comfortable with your true self, in all its imperfect glory, will enable you to be far more supportive of others—diminishing any urge to compete.

In this final section, we're going to look at *all* of this. We'll look at what we're doing well and, also, at ways we can help ourselves do better. You'll hopefully grow more confident as you identify your own strengths and realize the value you offer to future friends. *Yes, you!* We'll dig into where and how to build real friendships in your own community and learn some discernment tools—not all barriers are permanent, and some bridges lead to pleasant people who may not be great friend material for you, and that's OK. With a better understanding of what's going on inside of you, a broadened perspective on the opportunities around you and solid ideas on how you, personally, can build connection and begin growing new friendships, you'll be ready to make things better for yourself and other women around you who are still wondering where to start.

This is for you. *And* it's for you to give to others.

Connection Point

We're all looking for the same things: respect, kindness, and to feel included and accepted. We want to be better human beings and to find friends who will facilitate our best intentions but still get a little silly and laugh with us along the way! We need "easy"—no guessing or interpreting. No eggshell walks to avoid hurting sensitive feelings and no walks over burning coals with an unstable, emotionally volatile person either. Just give us a companionable, side-by-side stroll with others who know and accept us "as is" and who delight in our company.

Connection bridges are solid character traits and values that make others feel safe, comfortable, and valued. They create an atmosphere conducive to the sharing of personal information and revelation of self—to the birth of friendship. Secure and connected, you're then free to develop the upper tier aspects of who you want to be, to begin fulfilling your greater potential, *and* you can actively support your new friends as they do the same thing.

I *love* how this works! Don't you?

Connecting Thoughts:

I am *not* going to freak out over any mistakes I may have made. It is mathematically, psychologically, historically, and ridiculously impossible for any of us to get a perfect score. Instead, I'm going to be more aware of how my thoughts turn into words and actions and give myself the opportunity to choose. Some easy things I can try are to avoid interrupting others, to make actual eye-to-eye contact with others, and to listen with full attention, hopefully finding follow-up questions I can ask that relate to what has been shared. I will actively seek to build the bridge qualities that enable good friend connections.

My Barriers to Bulldoze: Where would you place your orange barrels? In what ways can you improve your ability to connect with others?

1. Sometimes, I find myself repeating things that would hurt others if revealed. I need to watch my mouth a little better.
2. I often feel nervous and self-conscious in social situations and worry what others will think of me. Sometimes, I find myself saying things to make myself sound smarter and more accomplished so that others will like me more. This doesn't work. I'd rather turn my focus to finding out about others when I meet them.
3. I tend to zero in on the worst possible scenario and spend a lot of time trying to avoid bad outcomes. This grows my anxiety and makes me sad and afraid. I will do better if I can identify and appreciate good things as they occur and focus only on *my* responsibilities—the things I can control.
4. I don't entirely trust other women and find myself wanting to make sure everyone knows where I fit. I'll fare better if I quit trying to land above others and, instead, try to appreciate what other women do well. Maybe I'll learn something, and in time, they'll notice good things in me too.
5. I can be a little thoughtless at times and need to work on being punctual and following through on promises I make. At times, it feels like my

needs are more important, but I want to remember that others' lives are of equal value.

6. When I find a good connection with someone, oftentimes, I want to protect it. I feel hurt when a friend spends time with someone else instead of me. I need to let friends have other friends, and I want to grow other friendships as well. I know this will lead to a better life balance than if I try to build my world around only one exclusive friendship.
7. I'm afraid that others will leave me and sometimes check or test relationships to make sure they won't. I like to be reassured that no matter how difficult I am, I won't be abandoned, but this is unfair and manipulative behavior that pushes others away. Instead of clinging to others, I will try to show gratitude for time and kindnesses shared, not expecting others to fill needs that I can and should take care of myself.

My Best Bridges: Where are you a natural builder? Which connective qualities come easiest to you?

1. To each his own. I consider myself to be mostly accepting of other peoples' views and choices, even when they're different than my own.
2. I'm fairly comfortable with me, just as I am, and don't have much trouble being straightforward with others.
3. I don't do drama.
4. I value and tend to foster long-term relationships with others. People know they can count on me to be a steadfast friend.
5. I'm a good listener. I look for ways to help others.
6. I'm good at taking turns and don't expect others to always choose my ideas first.
7. I like to let people know I'm thinking of them, and I'm good at making space for others in my schedule.
8. I've learned to laugh at my own mistakes and don't get offended when others laugh with me.
9. I try to ask myself, "Is it kind?" before speaking or acting. I'm very aware of the impact my words have on others.

SECTION THREE

Keys to Connection

Momentarily isolated individuals often create a lifestyle of unintentional disconnection with their own inadvertent rut-digging.

Chapter Eight

Attitude

Are you beginning to suspect that, over time, as you felt more and more disconnected, you might have developed a less than helpful habit or two? That you might have inadvertently become an additional obstacle to your own social connection?

You're probably right.

However, 1) you're probably *wrong* about many of the reasons, and 2) this fact also makes you *pivotal* to the solution! Which puts you in a very powerful place to begin creating the kind of life you'll want to live in—the kind of life other people will want to visit and become a part of.

Just as turning a physical key the wrong way in a door lock will restrict entry, your attitude, approach to others, and access to a connected lifestyle will either facilitate or sabotage your quest for connection.

Let's make sure we're turning these keys in the right direction.

It's all about you.

Um, let me clarify that a little. This *section* is all about you. Ultimately however, it will be about you and multiple people—your connective friendships. But it all begins with your own life because, whether you know it or not, you're queen of this kingdom.

Awareness of the Need

A few years ago, on a weekend the kids were away at their dad's, I noticed a stuffed lizard hanging from a hallway mirror. The happy little guy, in pastel sherbet tones of orange and green, clung with magnetized claws and a goofy smile as he had, I suddenly realized, for at least the past three or four years. I counted back from seventeen, Hannah's age at the time, and realized the span was more likely double that. Several years ago, she had cleared out some "kid toys" and tossed the lizard in the to-be-donated pile outside her room at which point one of her brothers had abetted its escape. Seven years later, the reptile remained, a googly-eyed plaything dangling on a wall inside the entry of my home. Definitely *not* a mainstream design move.

Apparently, I'd given the critter squatter's rights. While it was an inadvertent decorating decision, it had hung there so long, I eventually quit noticing it. No amount of back-stepping, museum-mode perspective gathering changed the view on this one. There was simply nothing artistic about this silly lizard toy. As a mom of two teenagers and a twenty-something, it looked ridiculously out of place. I cringed to think of the numerous visitors who had politely ignored it and then spun into a whole house walk-through that was quite revealing. *Why do I still have all these mismatched plastic kiddie cups? Is that really an elementary school lunch menu hanging on the side of the fridge? Am I ever going to use this BOGO miniature golf coupon beside it? That expired six years ago?!*

It was horrifying. I was basically living back in 2004.

With updated appliances and flooring, though!

Feeble, Heather. You've got nothing for this one.

With my new awareness, I could no longer ignore what would prove to be a bonanza for our local Kidney Foundation, Salvation Army, and Veterans Association. Problem and solution identified, charity pick-up days now gave me a giddy festive feeling. We would load our giveaways into boxes and bags, and I'd enthusiastically countdown the hours until they could be placed as offerings on the front porch. "Kids, don't forget to bring down your stuff! Tomorrow's 'Donation Day!'" It was empowering to make steady progress on my decluttering goal—and how cool that we could help others at the same time! Win-win, right?

Let's grab hold of that critical thought, because this analogy is a direct double match to your inborn need for connection: Once you *recognize* your need for relationship, you can help yourself—and others—*at the same time.* Actively growing connection into your life isn't a one-way charity thing directed at *you.* You have something valuable to share in return, just as you are today. Yes, you need friends, but your friendship is also a gift.

Sometimes we approach others almost apologetically, aware only of our own fragile hope. Understand that connection is a universal need. Your desire to grow friendships isn't unique, and many other women *want exactly the same thing*—to be a direct dial number on somebody's phone. To be instantly recognized at "Hey, it's me." Opportunities for new friendships are *everywhere* once you're aware of the possibilities.

Recognize your need.

Recognize, also, that the same biological need exists in other women around you.

Alertness to Opportunities

Adrianne and I often laugh at how we first met. Shivering through an early season track meet, I made a beeline for the heated women's bathroom after my daughter's first race ended, intent on regenerating feeling in my fingertips before she ran again. Bursting into the blast of welcome warmth—*a bit of HVAC overkill, but none of us huddled masses felt any urge to blow that whistle*—I stopped short of running over a woman adjusting a shoelace. Adrianne looked up with a bright smile, said, "Hey, I know you from LinkedIn," and thus began a wonderful, real-time face-to-face friendship.

Gloria and I met on a hiking trail—"Don't I know you from the gym?" Sierra, pregnant at the time, chatted with me from a proximate manicure station—"Is this your first baby?" *It was her third.* Karen came to one of my Barnes and Noble book events—"Want to join us at the Mexican restaurant across the street?" Marnie and I met on a dance floor, and I first chatted with Kathy as a guest on her radio program. Kristin and I met in the support group, and two Roses and Jill were great friend-finds at business networking events. Doctors' offices, grocery stores, dog-walking, Facebook...Once I activated my friend-finding radar, I began noticing all kinds of women around me who shared my yearning for connection.

Availability to Others

One of the biggest blocks to maintaining an open attitude toward new friendships is the Efficiency Effect we discussed way back in Chapter Three. Our need to squeeze the most we can into teensy slots of time leaves us hesitant—reluctant—to pause for unscheduled events and opportunities. Ideally, we'd share a laugh with a stranger, think, *'She might be a fun friend'* and then simply DVR-record a future meeting to play out at our convenience, *if and when there's nothing better going on.* But treasure hunters don't get to choose when they strike gold, do they?

Eileen and I owe our friendship to some leftover Halloween candy. We'd been introduced in passing at our gym and could have easily relegated that first polite "hello" to ongoing casual nods and "nice weather" comments. Lucky for us, she happened to be walking by when my pre-workout candy bar—*the only edible to be found in my car*—left me spinning my legs like a cartoon character flying off the side of a cliff. "Hi, um, Eileen, is it? I think I'm about to pass out." It was a little abrupt, but she slid down to lean against the nearest wall with me, and we lost track of time, chatting as I recovered. Our spontaneous, serendipitous connection grew into a fast friendship and shared journey through relationships, health issues, and career changes with a whole lot of priceless laughter along the way.

If Eileen had been in a hurry to finish her own exercise or wrapped up in answering text messages—or uninterested in women who made questionable pre-workout nutrition choices, we'd have been non-starters. But she was available at that moment on that day, and there's nothing like a humbling little medical emergency to peel back a layer or two and cement a random connection into a more permanent bond.

Being available to others may mean opting for a Plan B that wasn't on your agenda. It means allowing your brain to slow down and pause for a moment rather than continue its race on toward the next item on your list. It may mean walking a little out of your way to finish a conversation or letting your phone ring to voicemail. By our forties and beyond, we can tend toward rigidity. I mean, we've been living in these bodies and lives long enough now to get a few routines down, right? Those can be hard to release. If you chat with the lady at the garden store who shares your perennial obsession, you may have to forfeit your trip to the dry cleaner's that day. If you linger to talk with the new neighbor, you'll have to choose between a shorter walk or a later dinner. And you already had a plan.

Autonomy is one of the better trade-ups when we cross into majority age. It eases the simultaneous burden of increased responsibilities and seems a fair offset against the additional time now required for our beauty rituals. *Gentle cleanser, anti-aging cream, moisturizer...*We may have more to do, but no one's going to stop us from watching Netflix while we pay the bills or from ordering Thai if the leftovers are less than thrilling. "I'm the boss of me!" right?

But while it feels like you're *controlling* your life, inflexibility will actually restrict you to the limits of your own imagination and personal history. And as much as you've already filed away in that beautiful brain of yours, there are multiple people, ideas, and experiences that could further enhance your world if you're open to the occasional Plan B, C, or D.

A more fluid flow and flexible attitude will better facilitate your goal in reading this book: to upgrade your life with meaningful connections. Try to view friend-finding as a daily treasure hunt. Aim to *not* walk by valuable finds without at least marking the spot for further investigation.

It's truly a matter of activating your own "other radar," of beginning to identify the trees within this huge forest of a world. Instead of viewing masses of people—at the deli, grocery, or gym—begin focusing on the individuals. Yes, those people in the checkout line, the very ones standing between you and the rapidly building traffic you must navigate to get home, fix dinner, and launch the evening's activities, are likely to have similar lives with comparable challenges and analogous hesitations to noticing the people around them. Yet they have the same need as you for human connection. Notice them.

Somebody has to go first.

If not you, then who?

Each of us has something of value to share, and each of us needs to connect with others. Process that for a moment. I'm not making some blanket Pollyanna statement—it's a truth. Consider all the knowledge and unique experiences beyond the reach of your finite life but potentially available in the minds and histories of the individuals around you. Kind of adds a little excitement to the whole getting-to-know-you thing, doesn't it? Now, I'm not suggesting you're going to find instant soulmates, hilarious compadres, and genius problem-solvers at every turn, but they *are* out there, and we can't predict when and where we will meet them. It makes sense to live with an openness to these opportunities in order to avoid missing the nearby gems among us in a mindless race to *"Next!"*

To summarize, we need to be:

- Aware of our mutual need for human connection
- Alert to the everyday opportunities for interaction
- Available to develop random "moments" into meaningful connection

This obviously takes some practice. Most of us have spent years honing polite ways to *not* see the people around us. Saves time, right? Less awkward too. I mean, what could you possibly have in common with that lady just ahead of you, the one scowling at her phone? She doesn't seem interested in anyone else, and accidental eye contact might require a response, so you pull out your phone too. *Did I get a text? Wonder if it's going to rain tomorrow...or next week then.* Before you know it, you've liked seven Facebook posts and are rethinking your pasta purchase on the conveyor belt—*So many good quinoa recipes, and I should definitely have looked a little harder for the bulgur wheat*—until you're the one scowling at a phone screen.

Choosing Engagement

To replace the status quo defaults that were so effective in keeping me safe but isolated, I incorporated some basic principles more in keeping with my goal of living a connected life. These steps help me maintain an essential openness to others; they act as filters for my thoughts and actions, enabling a more natural flow toward every day connections.

Ready? They're simple but very effective!

1. **Smile and make eye contact. Say hi.**
   Let me actively work to better my corner of the world by communicating, "I see you."
2. **Remember that he/she is doing their best.**
   I choose to believe that everyone is doing the best they can with the tools they have available to them at this moment. I may not agree with their choices, but unless they cause harm, the decisions are theirs to make.
3. **Discover the hidden bonus.**
   Just like me, this is someone's son or daughter, with unique perspectives, experiences, skills, and talents—different from my own, and therefore, of value to me in my quest to learn and understand.
4. **Pause for pedestrians; make way for the merge.**
   Let me never be in such a hurry that I'm oblivious to the needs of others.

Can you see how these tend to shift focus toward appreciating the lives of the strangers around you? Now, I obviously can't let *every* car into traffic, or I'd be doing a grave disservice to all those behind me. And yes, it's a challenge to pause for even one when I'm running late, but I do it anyway—knowing that a few additional seconds won't noticeably impact my outcome and that maintaining my awareness of others will adjust my focus in a more positive direction *and* make someone else's day a little bit better. *Which makes my day a little better too!*

The Ruts

Loneliness can easily throw us into survival mode. As Dr. Cacioppo explains in *Loneliness: Human Nature and the Need for Social Connection,* we're *programmed* for interaction with others! Social groups and relationships have been fundamental to human survival, and early moms relied on one another for far bigger things than crockpot recipes and soccer practice pickup. Back then, survival of the fittest had *nothing* to do with spinning class and *everything* to do with alerting one another to threats from nature and hostile enemies.

A time of isolation can readily stir up those primitive responses. When we feel socially excluded, we start scanning for confirming evidence and snap into hyper-arousal with amped up epinephrine (adrenaline) levels and a revved up cardiovascular response: *Alert! Alert! Possible rejection ahead!*

Think "hot yoga," but without any redeeming health benefits.

Feeling disconnected and lonely even disrupts the way we process social signals.[35] The increased anxiety—*"Fight or Flight," anyone?*—impacts our body chemistry and cognitive function, downgrading the *accuracy* of our perceptions and interpretations. With no helpful, *alternate* perspectives available to us, obstacles loom larger and closer, as if we're viewing them all in a car's rear view mirror. Successes, on the other hand, fizzle down to more trivial, neutral events. *I'm King of the molehill. Sigh.* The world looks scary. Unfriendly. More than we can handle.

We grow overly sensitive to innocuous details, actively developing our own miserably distorted reality. And if life is loaded with Facebook friends or bursting with activity, we're likely to misidentify the root problem, thinking, *"There's something wrong with me!"* versus the true situation: The quantity and/or quality of my relationships is inadequate to feed my personal needs for meaningful connection.

As you'd expect, defining yourself as less than adequate activates all sorts of emotional defenses. If your target of engagement seems less than immediately responsive, your focus will understandably shift toward protection, shutting down genuine openness and dimming that friendly "Great to meet you!" down to a merely polite "Hello."

Do you see how easily we can get pinned by our own bad assumptions and fears?

Our natural, intense hunger for connection, contrasted against a social void, can *easily* drive us toward counterproductive behaviors that work together to create even *more* distance. These responses become instinctive, deployed before we've even arrived at "hello," and they develop into ruts that trap us away from the connection we so desperately need to thrive. Momentarily isolated individuals often create a lifestyle of unintentional disconnection with their own inadvertent rut-digging.

As understandable as many of these innate responses may be, they're completely unhelpful and can be a major factor in extending a difficult and lonely *transitional* event into a state of *chronic* loneliness. Because they're instinctive and can seem right, we must be hyper-aware of any tendencies we may have developed and be prepared to make on-the-spot substitutions for erroneous thoughts and isolating actions. Here are some of the big ones.

1) Playing the Translator.

Some of you just *love* to figure things out. You may have direct-from-God navigation skills—*"No, you'll want to turn here so you can get on the freeway faster."* Or maybe you moonlight as a movie forecaster—*"She's really his mother! And he's going to find her name in that box of letters!"* And it's *really* hard not to do the same with people. You want to understand so that you can prepare, right? Maybe you grew up in a home where "It's fine" meant trouble later, and anger was buried in silence. You had to navigate hidden undercurrents or risk emotional or physical harm.

I get that. But you're an adult now, and it isn't normal or healthy to mask or misrepresent the truth, so it's time to move on. We recognized genuineness as an essential bridge to connection in Chapter Seven; this is a two-way traverse. We present our authentic selves to others, *and* we expect that others are doing the same.

Will they do it all the time? Will others always say what they mean?

Of course not. But that's not the point. You're simply handing them back their own responsibility. It was never yours to begin with, and quite honestly, you have plenty to do already, don't you? If you're constantly playing Pin-the-Feeling-on-the-Friend, where will you then draw the line?

But what if someone is obviously upset? What if someone seems annoyed?

Bring it to the surface. Simply ask: "Is something upsetting you?" or "Have I offended you in some way?" or "Is this a good time to talk?" And then listen. If the response is another "No, it's fine," or *"sniff, sniff"* or *"huff, puff"*—then so be it. You've done your due diligence. You are *not* Project Manager—we're skipping those emotional excavation projects, remember?

Alternative Choice: *Face Value = Fair Value*

Value your intuition because it's a very valuable gift., but don't rely on it. The adult reality is that we must each speak for our own self. No telling someone else something you *hope* they'll share with another because you aren't comfortable saying the words. No leading questions or veiled emails. Just the tactful truth, straight up.

Instead of guessing or ascribing intention to another, assume their integrity—*unless proven otherwise, in which case, you are free to steer clear in the future.* This respects their adulthood. Kindly say what you mean and mean what you say, and trust that that *their* words match *their* truth. Another grownup's passive-aggressive or evasive communication is not your responsibility. Taking a firm line on this demonstrates confident maturity. You can't solve it, so don't waste your energy trying to dig them out of their rut.

2) The Negative Default.

Our reflexive reactions will either improve a difficult social condition and help satiate that hunger for connection *or* spiral us further down toward extended isolation. As noted earlier, when we're disconnected, these guiding instincts—that will either mobilize or disable us—are more likely to be based on imperfect perceptions. Distortions in our processing and interpretation of social cues, combined with funhouse-mirror views of ourselves and others, can lead us to follow falsely-construed fiction as a factual path.

Even if you've determined not to be *vocally* negative and stand ready to spin sunshine into every conversation, loneliness can still act as a dimming filter, adversely affecting the ambience, nuances, and tonal qualities of the world around you. Yes, even *unexpressed* negativity is a mirage-maker! It can warp your perspective as if you're the star player in a VR battle game who must be hyper-alert to perceived threats and fully prepared to fend off phantom enemies. Viewing social situations as potential minefields will shift one's focus toward avoidance and defense—when the reality is more likely to be a roomful of mildly bored or distracted adults who would welcome genuine interaction with someone like you or me.

A negative default tendency—pessimism—leads us to fast forward to the "inevitable" worst-case conclusion to avoid any painful surprises. The brain does a better-just-get-it-over-with polar bear plunge, even while there are still any number of less tortuous and potentially pleasant alternatives in the vicinity. It imposes a false truth over a still fluid situation, freezing it on "fail." When avoidance then becomes one's life strategy, it twists resilience into defeatism.

Alternative Choice: *Consider the other possibilities.*

Anytime you're tempted toward a negative judgment, challenge yourself to come up with at least three alternative endings or explanations.

Example: You spot a work contact or parent from your child's school outside your normal context—perhaps, she's sharing a booth with a lunch companion in a casual restaurant and within your path to the available seating. You approach, ready with an expectant smile, but her eyes simply roll over and past you. *Did she just snub me?!* You have a choice here: Jump to a negative conclusion—or appreciate the limits of your own knowledge.

It's possible she truly didn't see you because a) She's nearsighted and forgot to wear her contact lenses. *Done that!* b) She's completely engrossed in the conversation. *Good for her on ignoring her cell phone notifications!* c) She's distracted by her own discomfort: a broken zipper, bunched undies, or an upset stomach.

Perhaps she did see you but a) She's with a client or on a tight schedule. *Yeah, she could have glanced up and said, "Nice to see you," but let's give her a little grace, shall we?* b) She blanked out on your name. *Again, a little grace?* c) She feels it would be rude or awkward to break the conversational flow. *Frankly, that deserves a little mental applause.* d) She intended to say "hi" momentarily, got wrapped up in a thought, and forgot. *If you've ever mission-aborted because you completely forgot the mission once you walked into the room, your house is glass!* Or e) She saw you and ignored you because she doesn't like you. *Drum roll...SO WHAT? Nobody is universally liked. Better that you like yourself than keep score on everyone else.*

Btw, if it was important to you, why didn't *you* initiate a greeting?

Remember that "obvious" is often only obvious to you.

3) No Room for Errors.

While a negative person expects or feels the need to prepare for a *bad* result, the perfectionist expects nothing but the *best* and is continually disappointed by anything less. Whether inborn, engrained, or some merged combination of genetics and environment, some of us carry around a whole system of weights and measures by which to quantify and qualify people and events. We've often tested them out on ourselves first, which makes it *seem* acceptable—*after all, we're not asking anyone to jump any hoop we wouldn't launch through ourselves*—but unbridled perfectionism aimed in *any* direction is innately harmful to relationships because it distracts us from true connection.

Its relentless demands create an environment of "not good enough" with no Bell curve mercy, prompting others more toward concealment than heart-to-heart revelation. And on a personal level, perfectionism can be *paralyzing* with the fear of failure leading to procrastination—further downgrading the whole perfectionist experience with additional guilt and a late start. No fun.

I finally had to broom smack this overbearing monster when it grew a bit *too* helpful at pointing out what was missing or not *quite* up to par. It was interfering with my enjoyment of what was "pretty darn good," as well as my ability, at times, to improve. Accustomed to accommodating, people-pleasing, and bent on earning a little more love, I knew that—if I could just do *this, that,* and *the other* thing—life would be *fantastic!* But *this, that,* and *the other* were mobile and morphing marks. My lofty bull's-eyes were misguided attempts to create order amidst some rather messy emotions. It would have saved a lot of time and trouble to clean up the emotional stuff first, but I dallied with these manufactured obsessions instead, which allowed me to fill any reflective time with ruminations on my inevitable misses: Time that might have been better spent taking productive steps toward personal growth. *Aim for perfect, miss the mark. Aim harder for perfect with an additional ding to self-esteem, miss again (or score a hit and raise the bar still higher to ensure a future miss). Repeat, repeat, repeat...Similar to spinning tires in deep mud, don't you think?*

While there are times "perfect" matters (when you're baking or building, for instance) most of the time, "pretty good" is actually pretty great! As a former Type A who downgraded her approach to the B+ level on most things, it's a far more enjoyable lifestyle for everyone in the vicinity. My work matters, so I do aim for "perfect" in communicating my message. *And thankfully have great editorial backup!* But dinner? My kid's room? How soon holiday decorations go up or get stashed away? Micromanaging those kinds of details is futile and of low reward to me. So, I don't.

Perfectionism will *not* aid you in connecting with others. It comes with synonyms such as "nit-picky" and "critical," and emits the pulsating vibe of a dangerous electrical current. Whether self-oriented, other-oriented, or socially prescribed (by an overbearing boss, spouse, or parent), its accessories are tension and dissatisfaction. *Not exactly what you'd wear to a party.*

Alternative Choice: ***Ask yourself, "Is it worth the wrinkle?"***

Most often, the answer will be a resounding (and *liberating)* "no." Keep in mind that, over time, our internal thought processes etch themselves into our faces with the staying power of permanent makeup. The eighty-year-old woman obsessed with gratitude for the efforts of others on her behalf has a far more pleasant and welcoming face than the one who has spent a lifetime measuring the distance between her high expectations and reality. But this *isn't* about external beauty—it is, instead, about the brutally real manner in which our internal thought patterns are revealed for all to see and respond to.

Perfectionism is, at its core, an attempt to control the unpredictable. And we simply can't. Are you pursuing a specific excellence that is tied to one of your personal or necessary passions—related to your career, chosen lifestyle, or key relationships? *Or*, is it a generalized obsession over details? In the first case, please double-check that you aren't unintentionally inflicting an ineffective micro-management experience on those in your path—*Is it really necessary that your family adhere to one method of folding their own socks?*—and know where your own release valve is located. In the second case? You've got an issue with personal happiness.

Unvarnished Disclosure: The Invalid

As a non-smoker, Allison's lung cancer diagnosis was completely unexpected, and she faced a tough recovery after her surgery. Her friends were eager to help, but I had to push her a little to state any food preferences when arranging for meals.

"I'm just so grateful for the help! Lighter foods would be easier to eat, but I'm not that picky. I have this friend who—" She laughed, "*Had* this friend."

Writing this book, I had to ask.

"There were six of us. When Andi got a breast cancer diagnosis, of course, we wanted to help, but it got so *complicated!* One friend did an online signup for her meals, but Andi had two food preference lists we had to crosscheck for acceptable choices. *And* while she needed help at home in the beginning, she insisted on 24/7 or nothing from us, and we all worked, of course! We couldn't do it. So, she hired her cleaning lady and then pulled in a family friend who stayed for three weeks. At least we could still help with meals, right?

"Betsy and I went over with food during the second week. We met the friend, who was very nice, but we had to wait quite a while for Andi to make her appearance. She had to fix her hair or something. Andi always liked things 'just so,' even when she was sick.

"Where do I start . . .? Allison laughed. "OK, she finally comes out, looks at the food we'd put in the fridge, said, 'I already have some of that' and stuck it in the freezer. Then she saw we had wine glasses. The friend had offered us something to drink because we were waiting so long! Andi asked, 'What did you drink?' And I said, 'Whatever was open in your fridge.' She didn't like that at all. *Then,* she spotted something on the floor. 'Who did that? The lotion footprint!' She pointed at it. 'You need to clean it up right now.' She looked at the three of us, and I was mortified. While we'd waited, I'd spotted a bottle of lotion on the table beside us and rubbed a little into my dry summer-worn feet. Busted! So, I confessed, apologized, and used the rag she gave me to wipe it up. But then, *she called me back!* Said I hadn't done it well enough and needed to do it again!"

"Wow."

"It was really embarrassing. For *all* of us. But I *still* went back to help her. It took one more time for me to hit my 'never again.'

"Sally, another friend in our group, had dinner food and didn't want to go alone, so I went with her. After giving Andi the meal, we asked if there was anything else she needed. She suggested loading the dishwasher, which we gladly did, but then she had us redo it while standing there to direct us on the 'proper way.' Then she said we could do her laundry, but it was like 'do only these three items at a time,' and there was a prewash wiping of the machine, an elaborate fluffing ritual, and strict instructions on hanging and drying. It was *so* particular I had to leave the room before I burst out laughing! When Andi came back out to the family room, I suggested my helping with something else, and she said I could clean her closets. I said, 'Your closets? Why?'

"'Because they need cleaning,' she said.

"That was it for me." Allison shook her head. "It was really too bad. She had at least two more surgeries after that. I'm not sure who she ever got to help her for those."

Aim for perfect where you must. Do your best, and then, divest. The efforts of others fall into that range of "unpredictable" and thus, "uncontrollable." Clinging to the results, good or bad—of yourself and others—will only impede future effort. Remember that failure is not a definition of who someone is, but, instead, valuable information that can be used in targeting future growth.

Don't waste a perfectly good mistake!

4) The Hateful Heckler.

When isolated, there's no reassuring friendly voice to tell us, "You've had a lot going on in your life lately, but it will get better. Maybe you're just a little overloaded this week." Nope, we're often stuck instead with that annoying and often outright *mean* frenemy—the Hateful Heckler—who lurks in the less than lovely recesses of our brains, diligently pointing out every personal deficiency, disrespectful slight, and potential disaster.

Do you know her?

While her tone may remind you of a critical parent or disapproving teacher, she uses *your* voice to exploit *your* private vulnerabilities. She follows you everywhere, running a snarky play-by-play of your every move with black-and-bleak color commentary. She's sarcastic. Mean-spirited. If she says, "Nice job," she's just letting you know that you screwed up again.

"Really?" comes with an arched eyebrow and shake of the head. If she were standing nearby, you could tell her to lay off with, "Hey, I'm doing my best to get through a tough day here!" But she's in your head, so instead, you can't resist listening in to hear what she'll say next.

Sure, she means well. She's trying to protect you from all those future disappointments, right? Telling you that playing the interpreter and defaulting to a negative perspective is reasonable behavior. But remember, she's a *frenemy.* Connecting fragments of information and filling in the vast unknown spaces with discouragement, simply to rein in your expectations, is all wrong. *Her* logic says that yelling out "gutter ball" before the bowling ball spins off the lane will somehow cancel out any future embarrassment on the digital scorecard, but she's yelling so loudly, you can't even focus on your game.

I can't believe you just said that.

You're going to lose your job and health insurance after the restructuring goes through!

A face-to-face friend engagement or even on-the-phone friend might illuminate illogical thinking or at least help you highlight the alternate possibilities to your doom and gloom perspective:

"No one noticed. And it wasn't that bad."

"Your last performance review was excellent, but you keep saying you're bored. If you're concerned, maybe it's a good time to start looking for a better challenge."

But when we lack the social support system that allows us to reorganize our thinking in healthier ways, it's far more difficult to reframe, regroup, and re-launch toward the positive. It's just you and the Hateful Heckler going one-on-one.

*What's **wrong** with me?*

Trust me, the Hateful Heckler will always have an answer if you choose to keep her in your life.

If there's a Hateful Heckler in your head acting as your primary source of information, it will take a toll. You start to believe her more and more. Much like an exclusive diet of Facebook might create the notion that *everyone* is traveling, playing, and succeeding with better friends, newer cars, trendier recipes, and far more fun than you. Not true. But we tend to give more credibility to the biggest stream of information.

This phantom frenemy is one of those unhealthy connections you need to let go of. You're lonely, not desperate! You can do better.

Alternative Choice: *Monitor Your Self Talk and Shut Down the Hateful Heckler.*

Have you ever shot any of these zingers at yourself? Feel free to paraphrase:

Don't get your hopes up.

Whoa. It actually worked. Guess you got lucky on that one.

And of course, you forgot to pick up your jacket at the cleaners again!

Whoa. Nice buzzkill going there . . .

Look at that. You totally screwed it up!

How could you be so stupid?

You look horrible (grimace at mirror). (Yep, that really helped.)

Who *is* this woman? And what makes her think she can talk to you that way?

In casual polling, *every woman I have ever asked* sheepishly admits to this self-abusive behavior.

"I can't help myself. It just kind of pops out."

"I know it isn't very nice, but . . ."

Now, I've never been on a cheerleading squad or coached a sports team, so this is strictly a layman's analysis, but as far as rallying pep talks go—those words would motivate *me* to simply go warm a bench somewhere! Those kinds of comments show poor sportsmanship. And why would anyone trash talk their own team? It just doesn't make sense.

Oh. You just want to be sure everyone, including yourself, understands that you aren't perfect? Well, thanks, but we all kind of knew that already. Yep, in fact, I'm actually counting on you to be as human as me. *And I sure hope you aren't going to hold my fallibility against me!*

If your instinctive response to a negative event is to trash talk your closest living relative—You—that's messed up. Seriously. Yeah, we've all done it, but please, prepare yourself for some radical change. Heckling yourself serves no useful purpose. There are far better ways to motivate yourself toward improvement.

I chose to shut down the Hateful Heckler because when I felt OK, she nudged me with doubts, and no matter how bad I felt she made me feel worse. She said things I'd *never* say to anyone else! Hurtful, discouraging words. She voiced unkind thoughts and, frankly, made up a lot of stories that weren't even true! Why give me the worst of myself? I decided to try talking to myself the way I talk to my daughter.

I *love* Hannah. She's my favorite girl in the whole world (and with only one daughter, I can say that)! She's beautiful, even as a grubby, sweaty, muddy mess after an all-day hike or competitive race. Yes, outer beauty isn't everything or anything close to the main thing, but I'd never say, "Good morning, sweetheart. Wow. You look gross." So, I don't say that to myself either. If it isn't Hannah-worthy, it isn't Heather-worthy either. Instead, I find a positive. The easiest and quickest way to a more encouraging attitude is to simply smile, so I often start there. It looks good, it feels good, and if you make it a habit, you can effectively rewire your brain into more positive thinking patterns.[36] Kind words flow more easily toward a woman with a smile on her face.

How about mistakes?

When Hannah plowed down a mailbox on her way to school her junior year of high school, I knew it wasn't intentional. There was no gain in making my responsible and repentant daughter feel worse than she already did. So, I hugged her and said I was sorry it had happened. That I was glad she wasn't hurt and that it would be OK. And then, together, we figured out our next steps. When I mess up, I try to be similarly kind to *me*. "Well, not exactly what you were aiming for, Heather, but you did your best." Or "Oh well. It will be better next time." I no longer rip myself apart for my errors.

In fact, when the occasional negative comment *does* cross my mind, such as when I recently dug through drawers searching for a teensy but *essential* electronic dongle to reset my fitness device, here is how it went: *Why didn't you just put it somewhere you could actually find it again?* And then I stopped myself. Emphatically. "Don't talk to yourself that way!"

But that's not enough. I also have to make up for the damage. "You were probably distracted when you put it away, but you'll find it eventually or we'll come up with something else. Let's just think through the possibilities here." And then for good measure: "Good job getting that replacement part for the refrigerator ordered! And hey, you remembered to make that birthday phone call, and it wasn't even on your calendar!"

But I don't even stop there. After all, I spent *years* following a fake news feed! My selective filter had identified criticisms as factual reporting and complimentary feedback as contrived bits of fiction—perhaps, *tinged* with reality, but a bit implausible to be accepted without a pillar or two of salt. This wasn't *anywhere* near neutral! Over the years, I'd been flipping a coin and taking the non-winning side *every time!*

After tabulating the negative messages with which I'd habitually indoctrinated myself, I decided to be more proactive. I resolved to set the record straight and even pad it on the side of encouragement. To help myself do better, I decided what I really needed was a personal cheerleader. *Me* cheering on *me*.

At first revelation, as I tentatively mouthed a "Go Heather!" to the bathroom mirror, my words lacked force and authenticity. I coaxed myself into a do-over but still felt silly, motivated only to wipe a smudge next to where my lips had formed the words. *"Go Heather!" Who says that?*

No one. But that's kind of the point, right?

I guess I had always expected somebody *else* to say, "Good job" and "Wow, look what *you* did!" But as a single mom and entrepreneur with no accolades but for occasional emails from readers and happy but often invisible clients, my successes were most often quiet check marks, and that silence often felt like "not good enough." Without a boss to assess my progress, without a spouse's affirmation, and without a reliable network of empathetic friends, I lacked much needed moral support. I eventually addressed my lack of connection (as you are, with this book!), but even before that, it was *essential* that I begin talking nicely to myself, even—maybe, *especially*—when no one else was listening. I accepted responsibility for generating my own encouragement.

I started "good jobbing" my own successes for tasks as important as completing client projects and as mundane as making a grocery trip before resorting to chocolate milk on the breakfast cereal. I "good jobbed" acts of bravery such as saying "hello" to a stranger and even celebrated my juggling skills when I managed stressful days with minimal stress. Because none of this was inconsequential in my life—it all had to be done, and most of it had to be done by me. My cheerleading efforts proved surprisingly effective. The more I congratulated myself, the more I noticed my progress and could enjoy even the little moments in my day.

I quit arguing with people when they complimented me (at least *most* of the time). When someone shoots me an "atta girl!" sometimes I even respond, "Thanks for noticing!" Try it! With a smile, of course. Keep it humble but sincere. If you did something well, enjoy that!

Here's the thing. If you're approaching potential friendships with the Hateful Heckler as your relationship coach, it's like holding out a gift saying, "Here, but I know you won't want this, because *blah, blah, blah.*" It wouldn't be surprising for the recipient to accept it with a polite smile and then tuck it away somewhere they'll soon forget.

You are worth more than that. Don't pretend otherwise.

A liberal application of grace toward yourself and others will act as a protective layer against negativity, much as sunscreen shields your skin from harmful UV rays.

Fight the Heckler with kindness and a few rallying cheers. And keep grace in your back pocket, within easy reach.

Connection Point

Connection begins with your self-identity: The relationship you've built with yourself. Is it a good one? Do you enjoy hanging out with her from time to time? Or does she tend to bring you down and make you uncomfortable with negative thought patterns and anxieties?

Depending on the quality of feedback you've received over the years from yourself and others, your self-perspective is likely to be at least *slightly* off the mark. For instance, you probably take many of your best qualities for granted.

Trust me, you're far too modest! And you may have a couple of blind spots because we *all* do. It is also quite likely that feeling separate—disconnected—has left you with inner wobbles when it comes to reaching out to others. This is normal. It would be quite unusual if you *didn't* feel that way! Does it help to know that most women mirror some of your internal dialogue and feel many of the same emotions that you do when it comes to friend-finding?

Can you also see why it's essential that you take your own first steps?

Somebody has to go first.

Let it be you.

Connecting Thoughts:

As substantial as they seem at times, I could be missing out by focusing on the gaps I've found in my life. I'm going to work at noticing other people more and worrying less about how they see *me*. Knowing that others share my biological need for connection makes it likely that, more times than not, people will appreciate my friendly smile and a hello. *Hey—I'm an ambassador to humanity!*

I'm also going to try to be more open and flexible, to be alert to those in my existing circles I don't know personally and to women who seem different than me. I'm not going to limit my friend-finding opportunities with pre-judgments. Instead, I will grow my curiosity about life experiences divergent from my own. *I'm a treasure hunter too!*

I'm going to work on the messages I send myself, knowing that they shape my self-image and confidence. I will shut down self-criticism with a firm, "Don't talk to yourself that way!" What's more, I will actively encourage myself—even aloud when no one's around because I need to hear affirmations in my own voice. If the words are unworthy to be spoken to my daughter/niece/mother/grandma/sister/*(someone you care about*), I will strive *not* to think or speak them about myself. *I'm my own personal cheerleader!*

OK. Would you please think of something you like about yourself? This can be a quality or a talent, something that others have noticed or that is your own secret knowledge. Can you say it out loud to yourself?

"You're a great mom/accountant/hiker/conversationalist/cook/organizer/*(fill in the blank)*."

"You always try to be kind/fair/thoughtful/dependable/punctual/*(fill in the blank)*."

And now for some random verbal encouragement, not because of who you are or what you can do, but simply because you are a human being worthy of love and support:

"Go *(your name)!*"

I know. At first it feels a little awkward. But you do this for athletes, right? Does your life not also contain some Olympic-sized challenges? Anytime you feel challenged or a little fearful, please make this your new go-to: "Go me!" And don't stop there. Build your confidence (because it *is* merited, I promise!) with ongoing, solid encouragement. *You can do this. Really. You can!*

It's your life and script, so let's rewrite the dialogue with words that will move it forward.

Ruts to Rev Out of:

1. I tend to look for hidden meanings and sometimes wonder what other people *really* think or feel. That's a lot of work, and it isn't even my responsibility. While I want to be sensitive to others, I'm going to let go of all the guesswork and simply communicate in a tactful but straightforward manner and assume that others will also act in this adult manner.
2. I worry too much. I also tend to take most of the responsibility for failed relationships and awkward social situations and spend a lot of time replaying what I should or could have done or said. But my suppositions and suspicions are unproductive: They consume time and energy and make me feel bad inside. I can see how unhelpful all of this is and how my recent isolation may have tinged my perspective and impacted my openness toward others. Since increased anxiety and negativity are common byproducts to disconnection, I will actively monitor my inner thought life by 1) reminding myself that I don't have all the information, 2) generating alternate possibilities for the negatives I think I see, and 3) being prepared to say, "So what!" when my genuine self isn't received warmly. I don't need everyone's approval or affection.
3. I expect too much from myself and others. I think I do this because I'm afraid of *(fill in the blank)*/want approval from *(fill in the blank)*/ feel like I need to make up for *(fill in the blank)*. I can see how this gets in the way of my happiness and how it might be making life unpleasant for others. Going forward I will try to focus on people and purpose first. For example, if the purpose is to create a fun social event, creating disharmony via exacting standards would defeat that purpose no matter how "perfect" the final product. When I begin to get knotted up over details, I will consciously refocus myself on the big picture and consider how best to honor people and purpose throughout the process. *Is it worth the wrinkle?*
4. My inner dialogue matters. I will not indulge in disparaging thoughts, nor direct critical words toward myself. I will be merciless in enforcing this and merciful in my self-assessments. I will actively correct the Hateful Heckler and consistently encourage myself, even aloud when I can. I am trying my best, and that is always good enough. *"Go me!"*

Friends will move, change, and occasionally fail you, so it will always be in your best interest to cultivate new connections.

Chapter Nine

Access

Let's talk logistics. Where will you find these new friends, and how will you begin to fit them into your life?

I remember my own déjà vu diagnosis: *Friends! I need to find friends!* While this was a terrific revelation, it felt like standing with binoculars at the edge of the Grand Canyon and spotting my car in a distant parking lot on the opposite side. My "Aha!" was abruptly followed by a sobering "How in the *world* will I get *there?*" *Frankly, the twenty-four-mile Kaibab to Bright Angel rim-to-rim trail hike with its more than ten-thousand-foot elevation change sounded less difficult than the walk to my neighbor's house across the street.*

It will be easier for you. That's the whole point of this conversation. I'll save you a few steps here, and then you can fill me in on your best cooking/travel/shopping shortcuts down the line. That's what friends do for each other, right?

Lack of Contacts Versus Lack of Meaningful Connection

First, let's determine if you're *dis*connected or just *poorly* connected. Living within crowds of people without attachments can feel *just as lonely* as an empty house. So, which is it? What's your honest assessment? Is your main issue an overall lack of interaction, or do you need to adjust your focus to permit deeper interpersonal investments?

If while reading these chapters, your internal dialogue has included a lot of "I should get back in touch with X," "Whatever happened to Y?" and "Z and I keep *talking* about meeting for dinner," you're already off the starting line. You've identified stoke-able connections and are recognizing that they need to be bumped up on your list of priorities.

However, even if you *are* one of the fortunate ones who's been wearing her ruby slippers all along, and simply needs to click her heels—*or contact list*—to tap into the power of friendship, I encourage you to broaden your reach. Recently, after finding an ancient handwritten phone list from my kids' elementary school years, I was mildly surprised to find I was no longer in contact with *any* of the women who had once been weekly or daily connections. Some had moved, one had undergone a serious illness during the same year my parents died, and others had begun careers that spun them in other directions. All had effectively vanished. These situational or proximate friendships had been of value to us both when convenient to our lives, but transitions subsequently dissolved those bonds built around carpools and our children's interests. While a perfectly normal development, problems arose because I had failed to cultivate new connections with whom I might "click" and was unable to replace the fade-away friends who turned out to be seasonal acquaintances.

Did a tough transition knock you sideways like a rogue wave in the surf? Know that there will be more. There will always be more. Their ultimate impact upon your well-being largely depends upon how well you maintain your connectedness. Friends will move, change, and occasionally fail you, so it will always be in your best interest to cultivate new connections. Consistently and continually. *Sustainable* connection is our target—to make connection your *lifestyle*. This approach will generate fresh relational resources and is key to maintaining balance when the next transitions hit. Remember that old song, "Make new friends, but keep the old. One is silver and the other's gold"? Be an active miner for precious friendships.

Continually sow new friendships, so that you may always know true friends.

Creating Your Path to Connection

Let's walk through how friend-finding might work in *your* life, because there are multiple options and paths. Some of these will feel more comfortable than others, but you need to consider them all because efficacy will vary by community, circumstance, and stage of life as well as with your personality and interests. There is no right or wrong, better or worse way. Our only measure is effectiveness, with an overall goal of weaving meaningful connections into your life.

Grab your laptop and phone. Be ready to jot down your ideas and discoveries as you thoughtfully consider and search out your options. Go ahead and bookmark or dog-ear the corner of this page for later reference. Let's make this happen!

1) Take inventory of potential reconnections.

Who do you know by name? Does anyone with whom you once spent time still reside on your phone or somewhere in your physical vicinity? Cultivating a few existing connections may provide an easy entry point, so look them over with fresh eyes. What invitations have you recently declined? Think of the ones who may have reached out: women who mentioned book clubs, volunteering opportunities, school meetings, community groups...At the very least, strengthening some of these contacts will give you a chance to purposefully practice.

On first evaluation, my inventory was scant. My contact list included a lot of "Karen? Or was she a 'Kelly'?" connections. Locked into my own misery, I'd paid minimal attention to what was going on around me for several years. But my moment of revelation would be my starting line. *Even if it appeared to be outside the actual arena.*

2) Identify upgradable acquaintances.

List prospective friends amongst your casual acquaintances. Who are you drawn to? Consider your proximate and situational connections—the women you already have regular contact with: neighbors, colleagues, board or committee members, fellow commuters, or fitness class regulars. Who is a frequent "hello" in your neighborhood or at work?

Go deeper. Think about acquaintances who have recently undergone life-changing events. Some of these women are likely to be more receptive to new connections.

3) Examine existing affiliations.

These will include your gym, alumni or networking groups, committees and organizations, and church/synagogue/mosque/temple. Could you invest a little more? Get involved in a more committed way? Building consistent contact with the same people will be essential to growing your foundation of friendship.

4) Increase your visibility.

Do a mental scroll through your typical weekday and weekend. Where do you regularly shop, dine, or work out? What habits could you tweak to permit more engagement? If you normally exercise in the quiet of your home, consider branching out into nearby parks and neighborhoods a couple of times a week, or joining a group fitness class at a nearby gym to locate proximate connection possibilities. Some markets have evening social hours geared to bring in busy professionals. It might be worth forgoing the convenient but sterile shopping near your home to become a familiar face in a more neighborly setting. Look for regularly scheduled opportunities where you can build connection with consistent attendance.

5) Update your social media presence.

You're on Facebook, right? It's far from perfect but remains the most popular of our current social media options. Gen Z and younger Millennials are branching out, but you'll still find 68% of U.S. adults on the platform with 74% checking in on a daily basis.[37] Posting your basic information (high school, college, hometown, current city) will reveal contacts from both present and past (especially if you include your maiden name) as well as social opportunities in your area. View it as a map of sorts—it won't connect you but can show you where to *find* connection and organically grow your social circle in real life.

Keep in mind, however, that Facebook is first and foremost a data-gathering and marketing business which makes you and your data a product. Its unusual business model and international impact have created unique issues that won't be quickly solved (regulatory changes are coming in light of recent data breaches). It's a *highly* useful means of connection, but only if you use it wisely and make full use of the precautions available to you: 1) Use two-step authentication. 2) Never use Facebook as your log-in to another social media site like Instagram or Pinterest. 3) Consider using a password manager for *all* of your online activity—*I do!* 4) Pay attention to new features and security measures as they become available.

6) Select additional affiliation opportunities.

Look over the plug-and-play options: the existing groups and organizations that you could join with a little nudge to your self-motivation. Is there a local alumni group? Ski or cycling club? How about community or arts-related opportunities? Groups affiliated with your church, kids' schools, or even your professional interests? What activities have you thought would be fun to try "if only"? Must you really wait? What if you went ahead and joined a half-marathon training group, or volunteered behind-the-scenes for a local production...or even auditioned for a part?

Consider your genuine interests. It's powerful to pursue your own passions. Do you know what they are? Give this serious thought. These stirrings are within you because of some natural proclivities. Why not begin to develop these unknown places in yourself? The more you grow into who you want to be, the more likely it is you will meet individuals with compatible interests.

Don't wait for them to find you. Go *be* You—the woman you aspire to be—instead.

7) Do additional research.

I was shocked to find how many connection opportunities I'd missed along the way, as I passively waited for the world to pull me into social orbit. While our moms and grandmas undoubtedly had more obvious opportunities in easy reach, they did *not* have the crazy fast magic of Google at their fingertips, and with a little effort, you can locate several ready-made options in your area. Not much of a search whiz? Try different combinations of the following keywords (and add your own!):

What you're looking for: groups, organizations, events, clubs

Where: your zip code, metro area, suburb, or community (include proximate locations), also "near me" or "in my area" if you have location enabled on your device

Purpose: networking, social networking, business networking, friendship, meetup

Who (describe yourself/circumstance or life stage): women, over 40, 50+, newcomers, single parent, divorced mom, adult single, widow, new in town

Special interests: books, ski club, fitness, softball league, music lovers, arts boosters, painting, wine tasting, volunteering

"Atlanta groups, women over forty, events"

"Hiking, cycling groups, women, Oregon"

"Central Ohio events, adult women, arts"

Be creative! Your interests will be different than mine. *Cooking classes didn't even cross my mind.* Do a Google search, check out the websites, and then head over to Facebook to find more information on the local groups in your area.

You may find several Meetup groups in your results. Meetup is a popular international organization with more than 29 million members in 180 countries that enables men and women to sample a variety of activities, pursue specialized interests, and develop new friendships. Each Meetup is a separate group, run by a local, and shared on the Meetup website where others can find, join, and sign up for planned activities. Areas of focus range from athletics to the creative arts, from travel and volunteerism to various stages of life and lifestyle (divorced moms, moms of teens, career women . . .). Some are designed for self-improvement or professional pursuits while others are purely social. The vibe will vary from group to group and may change over time, so be prepared to try a few in your search for a few winners. *View the "not for me" ones as good practice.* Women have shared that some of the mixed singles groups with an underlying focus on in-group matchmaking can feel a bit competitive, aka a middle school repeat. *No thanks.* Be cautious also of groups geared to the bitterly divorced where concerted rut-digging can create a bottomless pit of self-pity and anger. Finding friends with mutual interests is great, but more importantly, search for similar values and positive attitudes. After all, you may have some yet-undeveloped interests to discover, and life is more fun with happy people! If you're married or similarly partnered, consider finding a group that includes couples, allowing you to share activities but also to develop independent friendships.

Some additional ideas: In their efforts to differentiate themselves from the big box stores, many local cycling and running stores now offer community-based training groups and weekly events. Look for and bookmark local online event calendars for your area and then check back regularly; if your inbox can handle it, sign up for notifications. Be thorough. As you discover local events and meetings, dig deep to identify the affiliated groups so that you can get in touch directly and receive notice of early event planning opportunities.

See what your local metro parks, along with any National Parks, Preserves, and Recreation Areas in your vicinity, might offer in the way of classes and educational activities. Does your community have an art or community center, a college or university? Search your chamber of commerce and local tourism websites for scheduled events, and identify the associated groups or organizations. Flip through a few of the ubiquitous freebie publications just inside the door at the gas station, grocery, drug store, or local library—you'll also find them on racks inside the entrance of many casual dining restaurants.

Libraries have had to step up their offerings to compete with our ready access to all things digital. Many have grown into community hubs and education centers, offering technical training, career classes, book clubs, and social opportunities as well as the more usual author events. Don't limit yourself to the nearest branch as some have been more proactive on rebranding and expanding these services.

On LinkedIn, use the advanced search option to discover potential networking groups in your city. While many will be web-only, there are likely to be networking/special interest groups that indulge in actual face-to-face meetings. You can often get a sense of the membership (and find out when next events are scheduled) by scrolling through the various discussions. Yes, this is a business site for making professional connections and that should be your first consideration, but certainly be open to new friendships that may develop as well.

8) Volunteer.

Want to feel important to someone? To be appreciated and needed? Volunteering can be a wonderful two-fer because helping others is one of the better ways to help yourself. A good volunteer is a real-time hero and often highly valued within a labor-strapped organization. Additionally, with everyone's attention focused on an event or cause, there's less social pressure. Check local news for upcoming events, meetings, and calls for community helpers. Many museums, performing arts venues, parks, and charity events rely on a volunteer base (and also offer free or reduced admission perks). My friends and I have volunteered at everything from charity golf tournaments and arts events to fundraisers and afternoons of community service. In the U.S., check out Volunteer Match where you can sign up by cause, group size, your special skills, and even age. In the U.K. look for The Campaign to End

Loneliness (which reaches out to the isolated elderly), Volunteering Matters, or The National Council for Volunteering Organisations (NCVO) which acts as a multi-purposed umbrella for its 13,000 member organisations/organizations. Here in Columbus, we have Columbus Gives Back, which pairs social time—a shared drink or meal—with service, allowing volunteers additional low-key interaction time.

Every community needs help. Your help. Take a few minutes to figure out where you can plug in. At the very least, you'll walk away with that satisfied, "I did something good today" feeling, and perhaps you'll find a "friend click" amongst your like-minded fellow volunteers.

Initiating Your Connected Lifestyle

For now, simply read through these next steps. We'll personalize them to your life at the end of the chapter. *You're doing great!*

1) Mark Your Starting Line.

Do you have any family or out-of-town friends who will support your well-being? Sharing both your need and your desire to fix a lack of connection puts that butterfly in a net where you can see it and call it by name. It may also open the door to some valuable accountability and compassion. My aunt and cousin provided essential phone support from the east coast when I identified my lack of real friendships as the source of my pain. Yes, it was embarrassing to admit I had no one, but I'm sure they already had a pretty good idea of my situation. If you're married or in a relationship, you may be able to enlist help from your "plus one." *And frankly, he or she may be relieved to know you aren't expecting them to be your 24/7 "everything."*

To speak the words is to make it real. This is difficult and painful stuff, and if you're anything like me, it helps to build in a few nudges to turn those good intentions into action steps. If you must do this completely solo, that's OK too, but mark your start date. *And you're always welcome to email me to say, "Hey Heather, I'm doing it. I'm starting my journey back to connection."*

2) Commit to Casual Daily Connection.

Disconnection feels *terrible,* but reemerging after a period of isolation can provoke some discomfiting feelings as well! This is normal, and even simple conversations may feel a bit awkward in the beginning. There were times I wondered if there would be sound when I moved my lips! We tend to overthink things. *"Should I comment on her jacket, or is that too much?" "Will she hear me if I say 'hi?'"* Trust me, others are just pleased to be acknowledged in a kind fashion. They aren't analyzing your "hello," so neither should you.

If you've been exceptionally isolated for an extended period, begin with a goal of at least three smiles and "hellos" per day, adding two per day each week until greeting others becomes habitual. Make eye contact. Smile. "Hi!" *You can do this!* Practice growing these little interactions into short conversations. Remember that you are sharing a gift. *"I see you."* Obviously, you don't want to get too personal with complete strangers, but a simple, "That's a nice color on you," or "Hope we can beat the rain!" are non-intrusive reaches that could develop into an exchange.

This is *not* relationship-building but is active practice to build your comfort level, confidence, and alertness to others. The grocery, bookstore, gym, sidewalk...the world is your arena. You'll never see many of these people again, so have at it. Be an ambassador to humanity.

If initiating contact *isn't* an issue for you, move on to the next step. But remember, those friendly smiles and "hellos" are a choice for active engagement and important to further developing your other-focus!

3) Take Facebook face-to-face.

Facebook put me back in touch with bits of my own history: childhood friends and high school and college classmates. It helped me connect more easily with neighbors and school parents. It also allowed me to practice connecting with a built-in safety net. *Hmm, was that post a little too personal? Delete!* In many ways, Facebook functions as the old residential phonebooks we used to rely upon—but with the added bonus of highlighting personal interests, hobbies, and mutual friendships and informing us about local events. As you discover commonalities and shared interests, you will begin to spot potential "clicks" and can use private messaging to explore setting up a face-to-face lunch or coffee.

Do *not* use Facebook as a window, however, unless you intend to go through a door. Beware of using it or *any* social media as a space-filler or as a measure of you and your life. If you're prone to media binging, please set limits for yourself. Be thoughtful, be discerning, and be aware of how social media use affects your mood. If you can avoid lingering and lurking and view Facebook as a virtual Rolodex and engagement tool, it can be a valuable resource for connecting in the real world. Use Facebook (and all social media) as a tool, not another distraction.

4) Create Calendar Priorities.

Knowing that my home had become my de facto hibernation station, I forced myself to seek daylight. And people. Few humans in my vicinity had any idea how lonely I felt inside. My inner chameleon had been diligently protecting me from those who might hurt, pity, or reject by encouraging me to blend into backgrounds and scurry for exits at first opportunity. Of course, this didn't make me very available to potential friends either. As a self-employed single mom, isolation was my effortless default. With virtually no built-in access to other adults beyond the occasional Amazon delivery from my UPS guy, Walt, I had to create my own path. And, because I knew I'd locate easy excuses when it felt uncomfortable—*I'm kind of tired; what's one more day?* —I resolved to build in accountability.

My chosen strategy was to schedule sociability into my calendar with a quota: two coffees or lunches per week. Occasionally, there was argument, and I had to boomerang my best tough-love parenting skills back at the source. *"Two? Do I have time for that? Wouldn't one be good enough?" "Whose side are you on here, Heather? Yes, two."* Initially, this felt *far* too rigid, but I recognized the greater good that would eventually come from holding myself to a "mandatory" social schedule. I had been prioritizing my fitness workouts for years. My social connection was just as important a health goal now and deserved the same respect.

Since I most often worked in quiet solitude at home, I added a weekly "remote office" day to my schedule too and began faithfully lugging my laptop into a Wi-Fi breakfast spot on Tuesday mornings. While not ideal for deep thought, the relative hubbub provided a lively and energizing backdrop for a couple hours' worth of answering emails, editing, and digging through research. I figured being near people was a good start, and it gave me a chance to practice eye contact, smiling, and initiating conversations. It made me feel more like the woman I wanted to be. It wasn't long before I bumped my single morning up to two.

Because I lacked people in a very general and all-encompassing way, I also talked myself into one networking event per month. I still remember walking into my first one. *Alone, and in a walking cast to boot!* I lived through it, realized that almost *everyone* walks in alone, and knew I was at least likely to recognize a few faces the next time. Progress.

5) Initiate.

You're alert, aware, and available. You've identified a few friendly targets as well as some groups and places that might be conducive to friend-finding. So how do you make it happen? *Gulp.* I know. This was hard for me as well, but knowing that others share your desire for connection should give you a lot more confidence. You'll get better the more you try it, so start casting out a few invitations.

Where did I find *my* coffee and lunch people? In the beginning, I simply scoured my contact list. Anyone who emailed or phoned me was a candidate. Despite my niggling fear that there was something wrong with me, I reached out, and over time—with therapy, some self-correction, and a bit of personal cheerleading—my self-image and confidence improved. The pivot point was my decision that the status quo was simply unacceptable. I would have to actively work to become the more social and other-focused woman I wanted to be, and this meant I would have to initiate. I reconnected with old voiceover contacts, began building friendships with other moms at my kids' schools, and approached business networking events with a dual purpose: Find new business contacts *and* seek out other similarly isolated entrepreneurs who might be open to new friendships.

Be real and be honest. *Remember, "genuine" is a bridge.* "I've been way too wrapped up in work lately and need to reconnect with real human beings again. Want to grab lunch sometime?" or "Now that the kids are in high school, I'm trying to begin building some non-kid connections, and we always have a lot to talk about. Want to hit a happy hour sometime?" or "I haven't had time to meet many people since we moved here. I would love to meet for coffee sometime." Then follow through. Don't stop short with a vague "soon." Instead, suggest a couple of dates. Be specific but flexible. If there isn't an immediate opportunity to sync calendars, trade business cards or phone numbers. I try to carry a couple of business cards everywhere I go. This may sound hardcore, but we leave a *lot* of floating possibilities in our wake. Try to reel a few of them in. Don't be pushy, but be decisive.

And if someone doesn't seem terribly interested? So be it. That's their deal and nothing you need to carry around. If they don't know you, they can't truly reject you now, can they? *And if the Hateful Heckler interjects, toss her out as an uninvited guest.*

6) Be a community-builder.

What if you were to create an access point for women to find new friends? Could you be the one to spark connection on a larger scale in your community?

Of course, not! I'll even list the reasons for you. Quoting from memory:

I don't have time.

I'm not good at organizing things.

I don't even know where I'd begin. Who would I ask?

People will think I'm pitiful or weird.

I'll feel worse if no one is interested.

Sounds too hard.

It turned out *I* was wrong. To my great surprise, I *could* be a community-builder. So maybe possibly, you could be one too? File that one under "food for thought."

Connection Point

As a nine- or ten-year-old I planted my own personal stash of radishes in our backyard garden, and then, in excited anticipation of my bounteous harvest, proceeded to sabotage both their development and ultimate size by periodically digging them up to measure growth. Similarly, we impede progress toward our personal goals when our loudest thought is *Are we there yet?* So, let's just go ahead and set up a timeline. Your calendar will alert you when it's time to peek at your progress, leaving you free to focus on what is within your firm control at this moment: the new habits you're building into your life.

Please write down today's date and your decision. Use your own words but write down something along the lines of: "I choose to build connection into my life. This is essential to my health and happiness, and I am going to make active, daily choices to help myself get connected." This is a love note to yourself, so leave it where you will glimpse it daily—on your bathroom mirror, dashboard, desktop, or door.

Next, build in your own encouragement by using your paper or online calendar to schedule personal progress reports. Write your own version of "Is it better?" "How are we doing?" or "New habits making a difference?" at two weeks, one month, three months, and six months from this date. These aren't end points: they're progress markers. By scheduling future evaluations for your growing connectivity, you will simultaneously hold yourself accountable *and* create space for cumulative change to happen. Knowing how isolation affects perception, it's important to keep your initial focus on meeting the daily and weekly connection goals you will choose for yourself. Feelings are fickle, and you are making some significant life changes—we want to rely on more than mood swings. *Don't dig for results before you've put in the growing time!*

Commit to your goal of connection and set your motivation markers. You know this is important. You will be accountable to yourself, because you now know that you must.

Connecting Thoughts:

1) Is there anyone I can talk to about this? A family member or a friend in another city?

If the answer is a "not really," that's absolutely OK. We're going to fix this. I just want you to take advantage of any resources you may already have.

2) I need to set some daily connection goals because interaction with others is good for all of us. Engaging with others can be as simple as a smile and "hello," but I need to be consistent with this. To build this into a habit, I commit to creating my own opportunities by going out in the world where I can greet at least three people daily, then five daily the following week, then seven...until "hello" is my new default. And as I notice the people around me, I'll also look for chances to engage in friendly conversations. I will push myself to accomplish this important goal for myself despite how I feel. It's good for me and will make a huge difference if I'm faithful to my commitment. *Consider ticking off these daily goals on your calendar if you need an extra nudge.*

*Set weekly connection points as well. How else can you help yourself? Do you need to schedule gym, library, or coffee-shop time to get yourself out of a cubicle or home office that provides little or no adult interaction? How about networking events? A weekly farmer's market? What about gauging interest for a workplace walking group or book club?

Consider additional calendar commitments you can make to grow your windows of interaction. *Yep, write them down where you won't be able to ignore them.*

3) I'm going to reach out to potential reconnections, upgradeable acquaintances, and social media connections with the goal of scheduling at least two face-to-face interactions per week. Every week. Some will "click," others will simply be a shared cup of coffee, but I can devote an hour of my time, two times a week, to go friend-finding in this fashion. *Please choose public locations for meeting new-to-you contacts.*

When I discover common interests in a potential friend, I'll continue to "go first" by suggesting other ideas for shared activities and be open to her suggestions as well, even if I've never done them before.

4) I will commit to volunteering and/or attending some of the groups and events I found in my internet search. Many others are also looking for new friendships. We won't find one another unless I put myself where these people are. Friend-finding will be my daily mission, and I will be alert and available to good, new connections. *Type these scheduled choices into your calendar as well!*

5) It seems like a lot of women in my area might be feeling just as isolated as I am. As I begin developing relationships and meeting new people, I'll try to be aware of who might be interested in creating a friend-finding access group like Cabernet Coaches.

Whether a connection will grow and fly on into friendship is irrelevant in the beginning.

Chapter Ten

Approach

If you've ever faced an audience under stage lights with middling to mammoth stage fright, you may have appreciated the blessing of not actually seeing most of their faces. You certainly sense their presence—*particularly during cold and flu season*—but those bright lights effectively bubble actors into the performance, allowing them to focus less on the audience and more upon themselves within the world they've created on stage. And this works well—ticket holders expect a *performance*. Entertainment. It would be a little weird for one of the leads to lean forward across the footlights and casually inquire if seat F24 has any fun vacation plans for the summer.

Our expectations are quite different in social settings, however. We're there for the interaction—and maybe the free hors d'oeuvres—but mostly, it's about being with others. We need to see them, hear them, and connect with them. If we approach others under a beam of self-targeted reflection, we lose much of our ability to do this. Distracted by the glare of our own worries and fears, it's difficult to focus on the faces in front of us and be a good listener.

This isn't revolutionary information. Your mom likely gave you some variation of "focus on the other person" as you navigated childhood. *And maybe that no one would notice your bad haircut if you just "smiled," which was questionable, but her first point, at least, was solid wisdom.*

Making it all about Them *should* take a big load off those high heels, but just as a bit of geological pressure will alter the composition of buried rock, a little social anxiety can squeeze that "other focus" you started out with, compressing it into the vastly different context of how *they* might think about *you* instead. Yep. We do a big pirouetting spin and make it all about Me again. *Oops.*

Fortunately, we can plan some presets to help us as we're getting started again, socially speaking. By refocusing your mental approach, there's less need to micromanage moments and thoughts, and connection can more easily flow through channels you've created for yourself ahead of time.

Connection Channels

1) Curiosity.

The Irish poet James Stephens shared this truth, "Curiosity will conquer fear even more than bravery will." Rather than stoking up courage when you're meeting new people or braving an unfamiliar social situation, focus instead on growing your everyday curiosity about the thoughts and experiences of others.

It's a matter of caring. Of stirring up your sense of wonder and searching for that "hidden bonus" we talked about in Chapter Seven. While this may be a more natural tendency for writers and scientists, *all* of us can gain valuable information from the people around us.

A political reporter once told me about meeting John F. Kennedy as a young boy. His dad had hauled him out of bed in the middle of the night to meet the future president in their downstairs foyer. "I had no real idea of who he was or would be and was half asleep, but I shook his hand—and then headed back to bed as quickly as I could!" As a sleepy child, his interest and focus were understandably elsewhere. The late-night meeting would gain importance only later when politics and current affairs began to attract his curiosity.

I remember also my oldest son's youthful reaction to meeting two-time Heisman trophy winner and football legend, Archie Griffin. When asked about it later, still under the spell of his deceased grandfather's rival allegiance (Dad was a University of Michigan Law School grad), Zak merely shrugged and said, "He played for Ohio State."

Often, whether someone else is "interesting" or not is less about the individual and more about our own level of engagement.

If you have trouble generating interest, view it as a private fact-gathering game. Challenge yourself to come away with two previously unknown details, either about the person you've met or in regard to one of their areas of knowledge. You win when you learn—*and have room for improvement if you walk away realizing you simply downloaded your verbal CV into the conversation!*

2) Calm.

Given a choice, when walking into a dog owner's home for the first time, most would like to be greeted, not by a yippy, leaping furball that might knock us off our feet, but rather with a happy tail wag and polite sniff. *From the dog. From you, a friendly hug will suffice.* Friendly is great; eager is fine, but *over*eager is simply too much, too soon. Now some of us *are* wound a little tighter, and vivacious energy can be engaging and fun; just be aware that without any developed context for who you are, a whirlwind approach can be initially off-putting. Give others space and time to connect.

At the other end of the spectrum, social anxiety, not uncommon after a time of isolation, can constrict our natural friendliness, drying up conversational flow and impeding real connection.

Your best approach to *anyone* will be to take a couple of deep breaths and look for their eyes. See them. Smile. Say hello. Speak their name. Notice their eye color. When they speak, focus on hearing their words over formulating your own. Be a listener first. If the other person appears uncomfortable, give him or her a hand by paving the way with a polite question or two.

Whether a connection will grow and fly on into friendship is irrelevant in the beginning. Don't add undue pressure with early evaluations and projections. Simply listen and connect.

Now you can engage in your treasure hunt.

3) Courteousness.

Obvious, right? But sometimes we simply aren't aware, and of course, our interpretations of some behaviors are variable: for instance, warmly hugging a more reserved acquaintance would feel like an invasion of her space and person, and a handshake, while never rude, *unless in conjunction with a sneeze,* might feel a tad un-friendly to a self-pronounced "hugger" expecting a warmer greeting. A little sensitivity goes a long way. But there's no need to prognosticate the widely varying expectations of others—just pay attention and be you.

Discourtesies most often arise out of simple thoughtlessness. When we're hurried or stressed, our focus, quite naturally, is narrowed. There's less brain power available for observation, and it's easy to miss details that would normally be obvious. *"Oh, I'm sorry! I didn't even see you!"* Striving to remain in calm, treasure-hunting mode will help considerably, and we all know the basic tenets of civility. We do our best to be on time for meetings and to avoid interrupting within our own conversations and those of others. We try to be attentive to the moment we're in, not scanning the room for better options. We're tactful and wouldn't dream of correcting a stranger's grammar. *Well maybe quietly, in our own minds, but never aloud.* We know that personal comments don't fit within a not-yet-personal friendship, and we avoid judging because we all have days we'd score below par on one thing or another. Easy.

Just be aware of that electronic interloper in your pocket or purse—*or heaven forbid, tightly gripped in your hand!* Don't let the Efficiency Effect turn you into a "phubber" who interrupts (*"Just a minute, please"*), ignores (*"Sorry, I need to check this"*), or seeks distraction (*What time is it? I wonder if Kerry texted back yet"*).

4) Confidence.

It is my dearest hope that, in addition to building connection with others, you are also feeling more and more connected with your authentic self. You, as you are, *and* you as you may one day be. Recognize them as the same woman, because we are *all* works in progress yet hold inestimable value at every step along our journey. Yes, even when we're not quite *there* yet.

We emerge into this world with a pure and selfish love of self. *"Me, me, me; now, now, now!"* Hopefully, Mom and Dad were there to feed, care, and nurture you. But for almost all of us, at some point, there was a glitch or a stumble. *Ouch!* And then another. *Oof.* And another...By the time we hit double digits we may have begun doubting our worth and launched into a multi-year struggle to compensate for all our perceived shortcomings in any number of ways.

Ideally, we then grew stronger and more stable and landed somewhere beyond all of that with an earned confidence in our discovered capabilities, and hopefully, a greater appreciation for the struggles of others. However, this can take a while, and experiencing any sort of isolation can be erosive to what we've overcome.

A few years ago, as I went through a box of my parents' effects, I ran across an old poem of mine, dated and framed beneath dingy cracked glass. Doing the math, I recognized it as the careful handwriting of a five-year old, counting down the days to her Christmas break. I remembered the words well: When my mom first read them, she immediately saw "teacher gift!" and had me print out multiple copies, suitable for framing and giving that holiday season. Reading them as an adult, I finally understood why. These are the simple words of a happy, healthy, hopeful young girl. Pulling the poem from the storage container, I could appreciate the eloquence and simple wisdom of my small self, and then soberly reflected upon the number of years it had taken for me to confidently speak these words as my truth again.

Me
"I am myself.
I am no one else.
I am just me.
Little, little me.
I like myself."
By Heather Dugan

Simple self-love. It's OK. It's good. We're actually *supposed* to like ourselves. We don't have to wait until we fix everything and become who we think we *should* be. We're unique and good enough, as is.

I am just me. Little, little me. I like myself.

Women need good friends. And if you ask me, they'll be very lucky to meet *you.*

Connection Point

You've got this! You're surrounded by *millions* of others who, like you, were built for human connection and face-to-face friendships. You've sorted through multiple ideas that will open new possibilities for interaction with others and identified some entry points for friend-finding. From here, it's a matter of choosing *your well-being* above any misplaced priorities, latent anxiety, old-school inertia, and excuse-making by simply honoring this commitment to yourself.

No apologies. No self-pity. No "same old, same old." Connection is *essential!* It's a two-way gift with far-reaching, broad-range impact. As your better-connected self, you will offer loved ones and the world at large a more energized, perceptive, motivated, and happy woman—and that kind of upgrade is of benefit to all!

Connecting Thought:

I'm luckier than many because I've identified both the issue and the steps I will take to solve it. As with millions of other women, my life got lonely. Like everyone around me, I need friends. In solving *my* problem, I can also help others feel more connected too.

I will focus on truly seeing and hearing the other person while I'm in his or her company and will strive to find out who they are. I can't guess which random connections will grow into meaningful friendships. I only know that many will, and that the more people I meet, the more friends I will find.

Life lives better, together.

Chapter Eleven

Upgrading Friendships in Your Community

So, not to put you on the spot or anything, but have you thought any further about being a pivot point for the women in your community? I fully understand any hesitations and even a desire to flip past this page, but as an accomplished foot-dragger myself, I need to share that founding—and finding—my Cabernet Coaches is one of the best decisions I ever accidentally made. DIY community-building to this extent won't be for everyone, but the factors enabling our success can provide valuable insight into facilitating strong member-to-member ties within any group you might want to tap into.

Unvarnished Disclosure: Upgraded Priorities

You can't miss Lana. Stylish, well-heeled, and elegantly-dressed, she's no wallflower, but it took some mental muscle to reach confident womanhood, and large segments of her journey did *not* include other women.

Adopted from a Korean orphanage when she was "two-ish"—"That was their best guess based on my body size"—she grew up in a small upstate New York town with no context for her ethnicity. "You'd never guess my blond-haired, blue-eyed older brother had also been adopted; my parents were your typical white middle-class couple. I had a very loving family, but my parents and the community in general had some old-school racist attitudes—just the times and what they'd grown up with, I guess. But there was no diversity whatsoever." She gravitated toward other outsiders in her high school theater group, including a couple of guys who'd been labeled "gay" well before that would ever be a socially acceptable option in their community.

Life changed with her first college roommate who, coincidentally, was also Korean. "For the first time I really embraced my heritage as something I should be proud of." After college she worked in New York City, married, and had a daughter. After the marriage ended, she spent some time back in upstate New York before landing in the Columbus area some twelve years ago.

I asked about her friendships with women.

"Most of my closest friendships have been with guys. Girls, and then later, women, always seemed to bring a lot of drama. Cattiness. Competitiveness. In girl groups, if you started to do more with someone you had a lot in common with, another friend would get upset because, 'she was my friend first!' That kind of thing. It would make me so crazy! I'd think: *Why can't we all be friends? Why do you feel like I'm taking something away from you?* I feel respect for *everyone* and just couldn't be a part of all the pettiness. With guys, it's more straightforward. Guys are really honest, more upfront, maybe overly outspoken sometimes, but those relationships always felt more comfortable to me. You always knew where you stood."

Lana jumpstarted a social life in Columbus via a couple of Meetup groups, but again, a negative experience with a competitive and unkind woman she'd counted a friend sent her back toward the straightforward male connections she'd grown to favor. "I ended up joining some outdoor/fitness-oriented groups which tend to have more guys, and a few of these became my new close friends." She quietly longed for female friendships, but on *her* terms, and Lana was skeptical of her gender's ability to build good relationships with one another. Ironically, it was one of her guy friends who eventually steered her toward Cabernet Coaches. "Rob had been to one of your 'coed' events and said, 'You really need to meet these women. They're different.'" It took over a year, but finally one Wednesday, Lana came. "I didn't know—*Would this be the typical women's group I've seen before, with women more interested in talking about their guy relationships than building friendships?*—but I was pleasantly surprised.

"I walked in around 6 and was surprised to see so many people—the huge table was packed! That was probably the most intimidating thing for me. You could tell a lot of the girls knew each other well and were close. I kind of wondered, *Is there still room for me?* But you were so nice. You came right over and welcomed me, and the women I sat with were so engaging, and they seemed genuinely interested in getting to know me. It was such a good experience and unlike anything I'd ever experienced, so much so that I said, 'I'm going to go again.' *Was that an anomaly or is that really the way it is?*"

She's been coming ever since. "At first, all the Facebook posts from women saying they scheduled everything around Wednesdays seemed strange. I'd never known a group that was like that, but after going and building friendships, I suddenly realized I was doing it too: scheduling meetings and dinners *around* our Wednesday nights, saying, 'I'll need to leave by 5' and 'I can't meet you until after 9.' There are so many different personalities, but we all kind of just mesh and *engage* with one another. Even women that, outside of this group, I wouldn't have chosen as friends because our drastically different viewpoints would seemingly create such potential for drama. But because we began within this healthy, *safe* environment, our priorities have changed—we all seem to value the friendships more than our own differing opinions. It's less about self and more about *us*. Even when two single women were both interested in a guy they'd met at one of the coed events, they talked it out. I was so proud! I thought, *'That's what **I** would have done!'* It really feels like a sisterhood."

Lana's theory on why our "sisterhood" grows and endures has to do with contagion. My delight in people in general, and the women of our group in particular, is no secret. "We recognize and respect that. You're so embracing and encouraging. It's infectious. We *want* your goal and purpose for this group. We want to practice that too. I think all of us—I'm relatively new; only a year—we love meeting new people and bringing them in. Yes, many of us know each other, but we want to give that same experience to every woman who walks in.

"I think most women crave female friendships, but if you've had some bad experiences, you quit seeking them out. You can live for years and never know what you're missing! These friendships have been dramatically different. They break down walls and let me be my real self on a deeper level than I can be with men. The bonds are stronger.

"With these women I'm finding new places and activities in this city that's been my home for more than ten years, and there's still so much to see and learn!"

Last night was our regular Wednesday meeting. With travel and illnesses, I *thought* we'd have a smaller group, but as is often the case, the prospect of facetime with friends is a powerful pull that can outmuscle even the most jammed schedule. Kris was thrilled to be back after missing a couple of weeks for her son's extracurricular activities. Jodi was pleasantly surprised to join us only two days into a new job. Mary just gave me a sheepish smile. "Decided to come, but I pulled over another table, so we're covered." There were at least eight unexpected additions to the evening seated around our train of side-to-side high-top tables, and that was fine. We encourage—*and occasionally beg*—RSVPs, but we choose venues that permit some flexibility. We'd rather squeeze someone in than miss anyone entirely!

While we occasionally meet in smaller groups of five or six at multiple locations, our Wednesday night "table trains" are the norm. Women speak of the energy and the feeling of family, how every arrival is celebrated, and that even when they drag themselves to join us after an exhausting day, they leave feeling energized and renewed. Mitzi leaned over to tell me that when another group moved their meetings to Wednesdays, "I had to tell them," she gestured at the women around us, "you're my people!"

So, what makes this work? Figuring out the unifying and sustaining elements has been a primary focus these past few months and the main topic at a couple of group discussions, because with understanding, our experience *can* be replicated in other communities. *Maybe yours?*

We're far bigger than a Wednesday night happy hour group; these friendships fill the rest of our weeks and lives as well.

Sustaining Elements

1) Consistent.

With few exceptions, we meet *every* Wednesday. Yep, that's at least 52 opportunities per calendar year! Approaching our second holiday season in 2015, I was *sure* everyone would be out-of-town or simply too busy, but several women still looked forward to gathering as a group, so we have no holiday break. Cabernet Coaches is, instead, part of our celebrations. *Our pre-Thanksgiving "Turkey Toast" has become a bit of a tradition for the over and under-achievers among us who have no last-minute kitchen obligations.*

This consistency is essential to our success because it makes us an always-available resource. Even when women are unable to attend for an extended period, simply knowing there's an open invitation every Wednesday can buoy them through a few back-to-back challenges, and if they've been a member for *any* length of time, others will note their absence and reach out in the meantime.

Many of our women knew about Cabernet Coaches for weeks or even *months* before their first attendance. They found us on Facebook or met another member; they heard about us from someone *else* who saw us on Facebook or knows a member. But few make a beeline for the next gathering. There's usually some hesitation. "*Are these women for real?*" "*Maybe next month.*" Most women simply file us away for "someday," and that eventual crystallization of resolve—moving from "maybe I should" to "I think I will"—can take time and be somewhat random. While our location changes weekly, our clockwork schedule makes us an evergreen option and easy to find even on short notice.

Cabernet Coaches is about friend-finding *and* relationship-building, and our casual yet regular schedule is essential to facilitating those goals. As women get to know one another over time, they discover those special friend "clicks," exchange contact information, and begin growing friendships on their own time.

2) Inclusive.

We keep it simple. All females are invited. Whether it's a co-worker at the office, a random contact made in an airport, or somebody's mother's friend's friend—the invitation is open.

Referrals come through both men and women, from ex-boyfriends and from business contacts. From those who have experienced the impact of face-to-face friendship in their own lives and from those who have observed its effect on someone they know. Women feel free to invite women they barely know because it requires no commitment on their part. There's no pressure to manufacture a connection if they find they have little in common. All the Cabernet Coach has done with her invitation is offer access to a pool of potential friends, and with the wide variety of women in our group, chances are excellent the new attendee will develop some strong connections on her own.

3) Accessible.

We frequent happy hours on Wednesday nights to keep it affordable for all. Some of the women enjoy more expensive dining experiences together on other evenings, but we strive to be budget-friendly at our regular meetings. And while convenience and menu specials draw us to happy hours, our group includes a few teetotalers as well; it isn't about the cabernet, but rather, the connection.

Also, when choosing locations, whether a member's home or an area restaurant, we aim for spots within an easy drive of our city's outer belt. By varying our location from week to week, no one is regularly stuck with an inordinately long drive (unless they live outside of the area completely).

4) Social media.

We're easy to find. In addition to our website, we're active on Instagram and Facebook. To enable both publicity—*We are here!*—and privacy, we utilize two-tier involvement on the latter. Anyone can find us through our public page. This is where we post most of our photos and notice of open-to-all events (which include spouses and significant others). Additionally, we encourage photo-tagging to increase our visibility into the additional layers of members' personal connections. Our group page, however, is private. Local women are added by other members or by sending their own request.

The Cabernet Coaches private group is our online heartbeat—where personal information and details regarding most of our get-togethers, planned and impromptu, can be safely shared. *"Who's up for a bike ride this Saturday morning?"* or *"Anyone else interested in this concert?" "I'm really struggling with . . ."* Members find real-time encouragement, inspiration, feedback, and support. Face-to-face is best, but our online presence helps prevent complete disconnection during times of physical absence.

5) Business cards.

I can't remember who first mentioned the idea, but it was a good one. Having a printed card with contact information and space to write in the week's meeting spot streamlines introductions to the group and gives newcomers more confidence to check us out. "Here's a great group where I've found a lot of new friendships. We meet every Wednesday and would love to have you join us!"

6) Regular contact.

Members receive an email every Monday that includes the location for our Wednesday meeting along with an opportunity to RSVP within our private group. The newsletter also includes photos from the past week, upcoming activities, and the occasional article or video on topics of interest.

7) Follow-up.

While we don't yet have a formal process for this, I try to get first-timers plugged in as quickly as possible. Women often exchange contact information with one another at a first or second meeting, and it's this spontaneous inclusiveness that reassures the visitor of our genuine interest in building friendships. Many times, newcomers get hooked up with our online group while still seated at the table and then forward their contact information in time for the next week's email. Connecting with our group can be—and often is—an immediate life upgrade. A woman arriving with an empty calendar can drive home with fun plans for her weekend.

8) Light-touch leadership.

While Cabernet Coaches began with me, it grew with *us*. My idea, but *our* group, and one that respects the needs and interests of *all* its members. While we adhere to basic tenets of inclusivity, kindness, and mutual respect that are non-negotiable, *how* and *where* we interact is guided by group members. *"This looks fun! Who will do this with me?"* I've encouraged women to post their own ideas, and as you would expect with such a variety of women, this results in a wide range of events and activities: comedy clubs and concerts; hiking, cycling and 5K races; yoga, cooking, and art classes; pub crawls and wine tastings; kayaking and paddle boarding; parties; festivals; travel... As we've grown, I've enlisted social media help, and members have also begun sharing responsibilities for our Wednesday night arrangements. The Wednesday helper-hostesses (Coachesses) enjoy introducing the group to their own favorite spots while following a very basic checklist to ensure we remain accessible and affordable to all.

Maintaining a light-touch leadership has enabled growth, keeps us relevant, and increases member investment. The less I sweat extraneous details, the more we can function as a team. Micromanagers get stressed—that's not for me. Maintaining a flexible, open, and generous perspective allows me to share responsibilities, offer a wider range of experiences, and avoid burnout.

Unifying Elements

Our fundamental bond beyond the one-to-one friendships is identification as a group member. We're "Cab Coaches," the "Wednesday night group," a "friend group," "my people/my tribe," or simply "Cabernet Coaches." The name is incidental—we could be Coffee Coaches, Fitness Friends, Book Buddies, or the Tea Tribe. But Cabernet Coaches has its own female-friendly culture that drives and defines us: individually, and as one. Here are what I view as the main defining aspects of our group culture:

1) Ladies first.

This is somewhat unusual. Many of us have traditionally and consistently relegated female friendships to a "bonus" category, to be included only after families, love interests, and careers. To prioritize them, and even place them center stage every single Wednesday night, is a new choice—and an important strike back at the Opportunity Clutter and Efficiency Effect that so easily isolate us. Our core members do their best to arrange schedules around this friend commitment, because they've simply found that their lives live better this way. Those who have husbands or "plus one's" still block off time with their Cabernet Coaches, either choosing Wednesday as a solo evening for both or delaying couple time for later in the evening. Adding a guy to one's life does not delete a woman's need for these foundational friendships.

2) Positive energy.

Our hearts are aimed up, with a simple awareness of how lucky we are. None of us orbit in a perfect universe, but we're united in appreciating all that is good about where we are—at this moment, in this day, with these people. We *want* to be happy, and we're grateful for opportunities to draft off the joys of others when our own week isn't going so well.

It often reminds me of a permit hike I did with the kids in Zion National Park many years ago. To trek The Subway requires hiking through a stream and pools of water and scrambling up some enormous boulders. By ourselves, three of us couldn't have managed some of those four- and five-foot river to rock spans, but as a group, we were indomitable. Zak (16 years old at the time) led the way, leaping atop each ledge and extending a hand down to his 5'4" mom. With a foot plant and a tug, I'd land next to him, and together we could pull Hannah and Matt up to join us. In this fashion, we trekked the toughest stretches, enjoyed the stunning beauty and adventure of the steep slot canyon, and fast-tracked it back out in time to beat the sunset.

This is also how we function in Cabernet Coaches. With our common goal we are willing to extend a helping hand or sympathetic ear toward those who need a momentary lift. No one pulls anyone down because we've chosen an upward direction. While I'm a key element of our group's positive focus, it's truly a course we select together. I'm never stuck alone with the heavy lifting. We climb together, and we pull together—and together we go up.

3) Mutual encouragement.

One of the first things new women comment on is the lack of competitiveness. Kristi said of her first Wednesday, "I'll always remember it. Allison got a promotion, and everyone was so happy for her! I'd never seen a group of women respond quite like that! Everyone celebrated with her!"

It's true! I like to think we function much like a healthy family: A win for one is a win for all. Because everyone is equally welcomed, all are similarly secure. Obviously, this not an enforceable attitude and occasionally a woman arrives, hoping to gather wing women for a manhunt or to simply advance her business interests. But we don't kick out overly-competitive women or call out those who might jockey for the spotlight; we don't have to. My observation has been that women will either choose to embrace the Cabernet Coaches culture—and grow with us—or simply move on. *And I always hope they'll return when the timing might be better.*

4) Generosity.

We share food; we also share our friendships. When women are secure in their belongingness, there's less of a need to be someone else's "favorite," and any hoarding urges are much reduced. We avoid the "Best Friend Myth," that childhood leftover that says we must exclude others to be included ourselves. By pluralizing our "BFFs" and "besties," we avoid the traps of boundary-building, instability, and any setup for future isolation. We expand our access to more of the world and can tap into the best aspects of multiple people.

Our structure facilitates the growth of deeper friendships while still including opportunities for all through our weekly gatherings and the open invitations that are frequently posted to our private group wall. While those with closer ties will understandably socialize more often, we've avoided the "drawbridge up" social jockeying of clique-building. Women in frequent contact often strive *not* to sit together on Wednesdays, sharing that time instead with newer faces. I encourage women to reserve exclusivity for their romantic relationships, and to maintain a *pool* of female "best friends" and acquaintances, because more friends will always mean more possibilities.

5) Welcoming.

There is no "typical" Cabernet Coach. We sit at multiple points on the religious, political, and socio-economic spectrums, and we respect everyone's right to pick their own spot. While the 2016 presidential election tested, and broke, many relationships across our country, Cabernet Coach friendships emerged intact. Realizing the futile volatility of stirring those waters, we avoided extended political discussions on our differences of opinion. While many of us do hold strong and even opposing social and political views, we worked to hold our friendships above it all as we waded through the contentious currents. It was the right choice. Going forward in uncertain times, our friendships remain a valued source of strength.

6) Vulnerability.

In a consistently kind, accepting, and encouraging atmosphere, women feel free to tell the truth—to reveal their humanness—even when it's personally painful. Personal revelations are safe with us. Last week, a Cabernet Coach disclosed the death of an old friendship that had included a blunt, "I just don't want to be your friend anymore." *Ouch.*

"I'm sure there are *many* people who don't care for my personality, but it took her twenty years to figure that out?" *Kim has a great sense of humor.* "With that group, it could sometimes be a little risky to leave the room," she said, referring to its occasional propensity toward gossip, particularly from the ex-friend, which made it all the more frustrating when her numerous efforts to find a cause for the rift and to reconcile were rebuffed. "We have so many mutual friends; she'd still come to my house for parties, but she absolutely refused to speak to me!"

My brain skittered between my friend's bravery in sharing her humiliation, to thankfulness that she felt completely safe to do so, to unprintable thoughts on the other woman's cruel behavior. *Grrr.* Such self-exposure deepens our connections, and it is the group's unity on maintaining a consistently kind, accepting, and encouraging atmosphere that makes this possible. While a difficult memory for our friend, the sting of the old friend's rejection was diminished by the simple act of revealing it, and in the knowing that her true friends loved her all the more for entrusting them with it.

Uplifting Undercurrents

Along this friend journey, I've latched on to a few practices that strengthen our friend-to-friend bonds as well as the overall health of our group. These concepts set a tone for harmonious relationships and build additional support into our structure.

1) Proactive kindness.

To actively seek out ways to help, encourage, and support is to take that extra step beyond "I see you" to "I care about you." Proactive kindness shows forethought, which is why it is so treasured—it makes the recipient feel especially valued. It is also specific, directed, and unexpected. Many of the women instinctively practice this themselves by actively looking for ways to add value into someone else's life. It might be an unsolicited offer of help, or a generous gift of time to someone in a tough spot. It is never transactional and always a gift. Choosing kind responses is good, but initiating kindness is the meaningful game changer that can fuel positive contagion.

2) Friend-matching.

Sometimes, you just get a feeling. There are commonalities in interests, experiences, or attitudes. *I bet they'd enjoy talking.* It's exciting to guide potential friends into contact. There's no pressure, and it's more intuition than anything scientific. It might be a gentle, "You might enjoy sitting by Darlene; I think you two have some fun things in common," or "I can't believe you haven't met Jill yet—you'd really like her!" I simply try to spotlight the more likely possibilities I've noted and keep a mental list of future friend-pairing suggestions.

3) Second-hand compliments.

While a direct complement is never a bad thing, mutual awareness as the words are spoken can lend ambiguity as to whether the statement was a simple civility or a genuine observation. The second-hand compliment cuts through all of that, because it is basically "good gossip": positive words spoken about an absent individual without the intent of it ever reaching their ears.

"You spoke very effectively" is great feedback. "Carolyn said you did a great job the other night," adds an additional weight of authenticity to the words, in the manner "Verified purchase" lends credibility to an Amazon review. I like to gather the kind comments of others and store them as gifts for future use. When Mitzi commented on how much she enjoyed meeting Karen, her words were immediately filed away for later sharing. Remembering the specifics, that Mitzi appreciated Karen's laid-back demeanor and good humor, added impact. I *still* remember Sally Bennett telling me—in *fifth grade!*—that Kim Maxwell was glad I was attending an upcoming slumber party because I was funny. Don't underestimate the incredible, long-ranging power of a good second-hand compliment.

4) Personal attention.

We are a group, but only because we're Cathy, Michelle, Tami, Renee, Molly, Christine, and Francie first. Cabernet Coaches is a community of unique individuals with a variety of opinions, interests, and experiences. The group conversations are fun and can be quite hilarious, but one-on-one connections are vital to our ongoing strength. As leader, I look for and create opportunities for private conversation, both on our Wednesday nights and individually with many of the women. My goal is to enjoy ongoing one-on-one conversations with each, and this is another reason for the occasional smaller group gatherings, to facilitate a deeper level of knowing for all of us.

5) Temperature checks.

While I eventually learned to balance my desire to help *every* isolated woman against her willingness to also help herself, I do try to reach out to those who fade from view. Often, a single communication or bit of encouragement is all it takes to actuate that still-growing urge to connect or reconnect. Other times, women are comforted merely by knowing they'll be remembered when circumstances allow them to return.

While less enjoyable, I've also initiated difficult conversations when necessary: perhaps a gentle reminder of our friend focus when a personal obsession or business interest conflicts with the social nature of our group or an encouragement toward honest, kind conversation when someone fears a potential misunderstanding with another member. We're grownups; I've *rarely* felt a need to nudge, and the situations have always resolved quickly. While a light-touch leader, I remain steadfast to our purpose, and this requires taking responsibility for the overall atmosphere.

Community-building

In a recent dream, I took a wrong turn at a football party and ended up on a starlit beach in a rising tide within a long line of immigrants seeking the safety and community of the happy crowds on a beach just above our heads. No one saw us. We scrambled to lift ourselves up the steep sandy bank as dangerous waves crashed higher and higher around us, but it seemed hopeless. Finally, though, one person made it up the embankment. She turned, knelt, and stretched out a hand to one below; and in that moment, it became possible for us all. One by one, with the help of another, we each clambered to safety and then reached back to help the others behind us, quickly building our own grateful community.

This is what we must also do for the isolated men and women who love separately amongst us.

Our relational infrastructure is broken, and the pain of even one woman—with its potential costs to healthcare, productivity, and family—will diminish the quality of life for her greater community as well. JD Vance notes in his critically acclaimed book *Hillbilly Elegy,* "We're more socially isolated than ever, and we pass that isolation down to our children."[38] His book depicts America's growing divide as a chasm that facilitates addictions, poverty, crime, and racism within its empty spaces. Author and prison reform advocate Piper Kerman observed in *Orange is the New Black,* "It wasn't just my choice of doing something bad and illegal that I had to own; it was also my lone-wolf style that had helped me make those mistakes and often made the aftermath of my actions worse for those I loved." In response to an audience member at one of her talks, Ms. Kerman noted an observable link between disconnection and recidivism as well as the rippling harm that extends into the next generations.[39]

Disconnection carries *many* costs, but the biggest toll may be on the children who lose part of a parent to increased stress and depression as they themselves absorb lessons on relationship-building from one who has forgotten how to connect and communicate. Our next generation inherits a vastly different world than the more social one we were born into. In this new universe, love is an emoji, tête-à-têtes are texted, and we coexist in online communities as we live in separate spaces. This inadvertent endowment of disconnection will extend far into future generations unless we actively value and model the alternate path: real-time face-to-face friendships and community-building. We need to leave a worthier legacy.

We are made for connection. Life lives better, *together.*

> "Mom was completely uprooted from her old life and deeply depressed when she moved here. This group made all the difference. It got her back into life again, rebuilt her confidence, and helped her find a new direction. Thank you."
>
> -Patrick, son of a Cabernet Coach

A few weeks ago, a white-haired gent paused by my machine at the gym. He said simply, "Thank you for making eye contact." He gestured. "People don't do that anymore."

I scanned the roomful of exercisers, many of them hunched over cell phones as they rested between weight sets and recognized the sad truth in his statement. While many dedicated fitness folks do simply value a more focused workout, a significant number of the averted eyes were merely scrolling through news feeds and text messages, ignoring the people around them in favor of the virtual world on their cell phone or TV screen.

Acknowledging Chuck with a smile as I entered the room that day was such a small thing to do, a simple gesture of civility, but it mattered. Now, we greet one another by name, and I know that if I do a mid-afternoon workout, I'm likely to spot his friendly and familiar face. That feels good.

Looking back on my most isolated periods, however, I well remember my early fears. *What if she doesn't hear me? What if I'm ignored? What if I get an unfriendly response?* I feared that someone else, through a rejection, would make me feel like an outsider, not comprehending that my own lack of action created the same outcome. The only difference was I'd chosen the guaranteed failure over the alternate route that offered the hope of change.

I'm thankful now for the misery I felt just a few years ago, because without it, I'd have remained rooted by my dead-end, wistfully eyeing a happy horizon and glumly wondering why no one had stopped to offer me a ride. Like many of us, I needed a nudge, and the unrelenting agony of my solitary existence forced change. When it finally dawned on me that my own feet could at least get me closer to where others might notice me, I began smiling and saying "Hi" even when I didn't feel like it inside. It wasn't much, but it was something, and I felt better for trying. Someone was finally helping me! And once I realized that so many others, just like me, wished for a bit of company on *their* journeys as well, it became almost *easy!* Because it was no longer just about me.

And the truth is, it was *never* just about me. Or just about you. Individually, we matter in invaluable and unique ways, but we can't fully comprehend any of this until we're integrated into a larger *us.* We need each other so that we may be fully ourselves as we're intended to be. And we cannot link communities and societies until we first link the individuals who live within them.

***

I wish there were some magical way I could have struck up a conversation with my long ago self as she sat alone in a parent meeting or struggled to get through another lonely weekend. To those around us in the school cafeteria, she would have looked like any normal, well-dressed, middle-class suburban mom, but I'd have noticed her glancing up from her phone at those nearby, busy in their own conversations and not seeing her. In my mind, I'd smile at her, we'd chat about one thing or the other, realize how much we had in common, and then I could say, "We should grab dinner sometime! Do you have any time for that in the next couple of weeks?"

Or maybe one of my Cabernet Coaches friends would spot this younger, lonely Heather walking Lily on a Saturday afternoon and comment on my sweet beautiful dog. They'd chat for a while at the side of a park trail, and then Kim or Debbie or Janis might say, "Well, I need to go meet some friends, but we have this amazing group of women that gets together every Wednesday to basically just build new friendships and socialize. It's really fun, and hey, just a minute...I think I have the information with me." She'd pull out one of her Cabernet Coaches cards and write her name, number, and our next meeting place on the back before handing it over. "You should come sometime. It really changed my life. These women are great, and I know they'd love to meet you."

My old self would surely have wanted to go and might have considered that possibility as she walked on with a bit of a smile, but her confidence would have wobbled. She'd have been a little afraid. And then something would come up, a reason or an excuse, and another week would pass. She'd have kept that card though, thinking about it as she soldiered on, pushing through a few more lonely weekends—busy, but unable to sleep at night, as exhaustion drained hope so low that stress inevitably seeped in. One day though, she'd finally work up the nerve to call.

"You probably don't remember me, but we met over at Highbanks Metro Park a few months ago, and you mentioned this Cabernet Coaches group. Is that still going on?"

And then life would begin to get better.

Acknowledgments

To those who entrusted the longings, hurts, and hopes of your hearts to me for the purposes of this book, thank you for bravely sharing the vulnerable and sometimes painful memories that have grown you into the wonderful women you are today. You are wiser than you know and have demonstrated the highest kindness by presenting your truths that we may all grow into stronger better women and truer, more faithful friends.

Zak, Hannah, and Matt: When you were young and life was a blur, I prayed for enough sleep that my brain would retain those fast-flying memories of babies, toddlers—Wait...teenagers? Already? I didn't have a great record with car keys and cell phones, and our fleeting moments were far more precious to me. They still are. We've traded sidewalks for hiking trails, Candyland games for some epic trash-talking Scrabble nights, and "mom knows best" for engrossing and enlightening discussions, but my best moments always seem to include one or more of you. I treasure our many and varied family experiences and thank you for your patient and loving support on this book journey. Thanks also for all the terrific analogies and metaphors you've unwittingly provided over the years (wink, wink). You inspire me; you make me laugh; you bring me closer to the woman I want to be. You are my favorite humans, always and forever.

Monda Sue Prior, Adrianne Benson, Kristi Hodson, Dennis Hetzel, Mary Byers, Kerry Novak, Barb Letcher, Kristin Smith, Kayron Charlesworth, Darlene Hallabrin, Debbie Peepers, Karen Kontras, Kim Moske, Kathy Chiero Greenzalis, Janis Frankenberg, and Allison Sims: Each of you provided crucial guidance, kind support, a listening ear, and essential encouragement. When I view the path of this book in my mind's eye, I see your faces at key points along the way and am exceptionally grateful. Thank you.

It took a news guy to spot the story. Many thanks to John Damschroder for first saying, "That's a book" in reference to my community-building efforts in the Columbus area. Where I saw happier, more productive, connected women, he perceived a movement—a self-planting and ever-expanding forest of possibilities—and recognized this book, still in my head, that might help others grow and develop their own wooded lots.

Cabernet Coaches, you are each part of this story. Because of each one of you, this group has blossomed into all of our best possibilities. It has never been about the cabernet but will forever be about sharing space and time in this world, in a way that permits us to launch beyond personal comfort zones into our deepest dreams together. A special "thank you" to the CC Wednesday night "hub": Barb L., Kayron C., Janis F., Karen K., Janet D., Debbie P., Tessa T., Carolyn K., Rose D., Jill H., Christine W., Molly M., Kerry N., Kris N., Darlene H., Kim M., Francie T., Kim S., Mary D., Sharon S., Terry W., Debbie K., Debbie Kr., Theresa L., Jodi W., Tami M., Sabrina H., Vicki D., Dawn N., Kristin S., Cathy S., Cathy Sh., Michelle S., Ann K., Bev F., Marla V., Jenn B., Lisa C., Catherine R., Karen P., Suzette S., and April C. And I send a big group hug to Marnie M., Carrie M., Gloria R., Barb W., Rose K., Mitzi A., Kristi H., and Renee W., who have left Columbus but never our hearts.

I'm deeply indebted to Marie Prys whose deft editing skills elevated my words and ideas to a higher plane, earning both my respect and highest recommendation. To Cathy Teets, of Headline Books, thank you for carrying my vision forward to where it may, hopefully, have exponential rippling impact.

And to all of you who asked, "How's the book?"—it mattered. Thank you for remembering, asking, and encouraging this author on through to the finish.

Bibliography

American Osteopathic Association. "Survey Finds Nearly Three-Quarters (72%) of Americans Feel Lonely." PR Newswire: News Distribution, Targeting and Monitoring. Accessed October 8, 2018. https://www.prnewswire.com/news-releases/survey-finds-nearly-three-quarters-72-of-americans-feel-lonely-300342742.html.

American Psychological Association. "Social Isolation, Loneliness Could Be Greater Threat to Public Health than Obesity." ScienceDaily. August 05, 2017. Accessed October 08, 2018. https://www.sciencedaily.com/releases/2017/08/170805165319.htm.

Anderson, G. Oscar. "Loneliness Among Older Adults: A National Survey of Adults 45." AARP. September 01, 2010. Accessed April 11, 2018. https://www.aarp.org/research/topics/life/info-2014/loneliness_2010.html.

Bean, Corliss, Michelle Fortier, Courtney Post, and Karam Chima. "Understanding How Organized Youth Sport May Be Harming Individual Players within the Family Unit: A Literature Review." *International Journal of Environmental Research and Public Health* 11, no. 10 (2014): 10226-0268. doi:10.3390/ijerph111010226.

Cacioppo, John T., and William Patrick. *Loneliness: Human Nature and the Need for Social Connection*. New York: Norton, 2009.

Cacioppo, John T., and Stephanie Cacioppo. "Social Relationships and Health: The Toxic Effects of Perceived Social Isolation." *Social and Personality Psychology Compass* 8, no. 2 (2014): 58-72. doi:10.1111/spc3.12087.

Cigna. "New Cigna Study Reveals Loneliness at Epidemic Levels in America." PR Newswire: News Distribution, Targeting and Monitoring. May 01, 2018. Accessed October 04. 2018. https://www.prnewswire.com/news-releases/new-cigna-study-reveals-loneliness-at-epidemic-levels-in-america-300639747.html.

Coughlan, Sean. "Digital Dependence 'eroding Human Memory'." BBC. October 07, 2015. Accessed April 12, 2018. http://www.bbc.com/news/education-34454264.

Crouse, Janice Shaw. "The Loneliness of American Society." *The American Spectator.* March 10, 2017. Accessed April 10, 2018. from http://spectator.org/articles/59230/loneliness-american-society.

"Data Never Sleeps 5.0 | Domo." Domo. June 2017. Accessed April 11, 2018. https://www.domo.com/learn/data-never-sleeps-5.

"Data Never Sleeps 6.0 | Domo." Domo. June 2018. Accessed October 09, 2018. https://www.domo.com/learn/data-never-sleeps-6.

Dugan, Heather. *Date Like a Grownup: Anecdotes, Admissions of Guilt & Advice Between Friends*. Columbus, Ohio: HDC Press, 2014.

"Ecotone." Ecotone - The Encyclopedia of Earth. Modifed May 15, 2018. Accessed September 25, 2018. https://editors.eol.org/eoearth/wiki/Ecotone.

Fleming, Victor, dir. *The Wizard of Oz*. 1939. United States. Metro-Goldwyn-Mayer. Motion Picture.

Gardiner, Bryan. "Why Does Stubbing Your Toe Hurt So Damn Much?" Wired. June 06, 2017. Accessed April 14, 2018. http://www.wired.com/2015/04/stubbing-toe-hurt-damn-much/.

Giang, Vivian. "How Smiling Changes Your Brain." Fast Company. January 30, 2015. Accessed April 14, 2018. www.fastcompany.com/3041438/how-smiling-changes-your-brain.

Goleman, Daniel. *Emotional Intelligence: Why It Can Matter More than IQ*. London: Bloomsbury, 2010.

"Holmes- Rahe Stress Inventory." The American Institute of Stress. August 15, 2017. Accessed April 12, 2018. https://www.stress.org/holmes-rahe-stress-inventory/.

"Home Organization in the U.S.: General Purpose, Closets, Garages and Storage Sheds, 4th Edition." Global Information, Inc. March 07, 2017. Accessed April 16, 2018. https://www.researchandmarkets.com/reports/4115664/home- organization-in-the-u-s-general-purpose#reld0-4229896.

Hopman, Rachel J., James R. Coleman, Jonna Turrill, Joel M. Cooper, and David L. Strayer. "Measuring Cognitive Distraction in the Automobile III: A Comparison of Ten 2015 In-Vehicle Information Systems." AAA Foundation. February 27, 2018. Accessed April 16. 2018. https://aaafoundation.org/measuring-cognitive-distraction-automobile-iii-comparison-ten-2015-vehicle-information-systems/.

Joelving, Frederik. "Why the #$%! Do We Swear? For Pain Relief." *Scientific American.* July 12, 2009. Accessed April 14, 2018. https://www.scientificamerican.com/article/why-do-we-swear/.

Keenan, M. "Alarming increase in Facebook related divorces in 2011." DivorceOnline-Blog. August 26, 2017. Accessed April 10, 2018. https://www.divorce-online.co.uk/blog/alarming-increase-in-facebook-related-divorces-in-2011/.

Keene, Carolyn. *Nancy Drew Mystery Stories.* New York, NY: Grosset & Dunlap. 1930-1979.

"Laughter Yoga for Health and Happiness." Laughter Yoga University. Accessed April 14, 2018. https://laughteryoga.org/laughter-yoga/about-laughter-yoga/.

Lennon, McCartney, Vanda, and Young, writers. *With a Little Help from My Friends; Good times.* Philips, 1968, CD.

Mcpherson, Miller, Lynn Smith-Lovin, and Matthew E. Brashears. "Social Isolation in America: Changes in Core Discussion Networks over Two Decades." *American Sociological Review* 73, no. 6 (2008): 1022. doi:10.1177/000312240807300610.

Maslow, A. H. "A Theory of Human Motivation." *Psychological Review* 50, no. 4 (1943): 370-96. doi:10.1037/h0054346.

Payson, Eleanor D. *The Wizard of Oz and Other Narcissists: Coping with the One-way Relationship in Work, Love, and Family.* Royal Oak, MI: Julian Day Publications, 2009.

Roberts, James A., and Meredith E. David. "My Life Has Become a Major Distraction from My Cell Phone: Partner Phubbing and Relationship Satisfaction among Romantic Partners." *Computers in Human Behavior* 54 (2016): 134-41. doi:10.1016/j.chb.2015.07.058.

Ronson, Jon. *So You've Been Publicly Shamed.* New York: Riverhead Books, 2015.

Smith, Aaron, and Monica Anderson. "Social Media Use 2018. Demographics and Statistics | Pew Research Center." Pew Research Center: Internet, Science & Tech. September 19, 2018. Accessed October 07, 2018. http://www.pewinternet.org/2018/03/01/social-media-use-in-2018/.

"U.S. Bureau of Labor Statistics." U.S. Bureau of Labor Statistics. Accessed April 16, 2018. https://www.bls.gov/tus/charts/household.htm.

Vance, J.D. *Hillbilly Elegy: A Memoir of a Family and Culture in Crisis.* New York: Harper, 2018.

Verduyn, Philippe, Oscar Ybarra, Maxime Resibois, John Jonides, and Ethan Kross. "Do Social Network Sites Enhance or Undermine Subjective Well-Being? A Critical Review." *Social Issues and Policy Review* 11, no. 1 (2017): 274-302. Doi:10:18411/a-2017-023.

Weinschenk, S. "The True Cost Of Multi-Tasking." Psychology Today. September 18, 2012. Accessed April 11, 2018. https://www.psychologytoday.com/us/blog/brain-wise/201209/the-true-cost-multi-tasking.

Endnotes

1 Heather Dugan. *Date Like a Grownup: Anecdotes, Admissions of Guilt & Advice Between Friends* (Columbus, Ohio: HDC Press, 2014).

2 John Lennon, Paul McCartney, "With a Little Help from My Friends," performed by Ringo Starr, *Yellow Submarine,* (1969, Apple Records, 1969).

3 American Osteopathic Association, "Survey Finds Nearly Three-Quarters (72%) of Ameri- cans Feel Lonely," *PR Newswire: News Distribution, Targeting and Monitoring,* October 22, 2016, accessed October 8, 2018, https://www.prnewswire.com/news-releases/survey-finds-nearly-three-quarters-72-of-americans-feel-lonely-300342742.html.

4 Cigna, "New Cigna Study Reveals Loneliness at Epidemic Levels in America," *PR Newswire: News Distribution, Targeting and Monitoring,* May 01, 2018, accessed October 04, 2018, https://www.prnewswire.com/news-releases/new-cigna-study-reveals-loneliness-at-epi- demic-levels-in-america-300639747.html.

5 American Psychological Association. "Social isolation, loneliness could be greater threat to public health than obesity." *ScienceDaily,* August 5, 2017, accessed October 8, 2018, www.sciencedaily.com/releases/2017/08/170805165319.htm.

6 Janice Shaw Crouse, "The Loneliness of American Society," *The American Spectator,* March 18, 2014, accessed April 10, 2018, http://spectator.org/articles/59230/loneliness-american-society.

7 John T. Cacioppo and William Patrick, *Loneliness: Human Nature and the Need for Social Connection* (New York: Norton, 2009). 83.

8 G. Oscar Anderson, "Loneliness Among Older Adults: A National Survey of Adults 45," AARP, September 2010, accessed April 11, 2018, https://doi.org/10.26419/res.00064.001.

9 Mark Keenan, "Alarming Increase in Facebook Related Divorces in 2011," *Divorce Online,* August 26, 2017, accessed April 10, 2018, https://www.divorce-online.co.uk/blog/alarming-increase-in-facebook-related-divorces-in-2011/.

10 John Payne, "Overcoming Information Overload in Decision Making," (lecture, Ted@ Allianz on Behavioral Finance, New York City, November 9, 2011).

11 S. Weinschenk, "The True Cost Of Multi-Tasking," *Psychology Today,* September 18, 2012, accessed September 25, 2018, https://www.psychologytoday.com/us/blog/brain-wise/201209/the-true-cost-multi-tasking.

12 Data Never Sleeps 5.0," Domo.com, June 2017, accessed April 11, 2018, https://www.domo.com/learn/data-never-sleeps-5.

13 "Data Never Sleeps 6.0," Domo.com, June 2018, accessed October 8, 2018, https://www.domo.com/learn/data-never-sleeps-6.

14 Coliss N. Bean, Michelle Fortier, Courtney Post, Karam Chima, "Understanding How Organized Youth Sport May Be Harming Individual Players within the Family Unit: A Literature Review," *Int. J. Environ. Res. Public Health* 11, no. 10: 10226-10268.

15 United States Department of Labor, Bureau of Labor and Statistics, "American Time Use Survey, Household Activities: Average minutes per day men and women spent in household activities," December 20, 2016, accessed April 11, 2018, http://www.bls.gov/tus/charts/household.htm.

16 Philippe Verduyn et al., "Do Social Network Sites Enhance or Undermine Subjective Well-Being? A Critical Review," *Social Issues and Policy Review* 11, no. 1 (2017), doi:10.18411/a-2017-023.

17 "Home Organization in the U.S.: General Purpose, Closets, Garages and Storage Sheds, 4th Edition," *Global Information, Inc.*, March 2017, accessed September 24, 2018, https://www.researchandmarkets.com/reports/4115664/home-organization-in-the-u-s-general-purpose#reld0-4229896.

18 Heather Dugan. *Date Like a Grownup: Anecdotes, Admissions of Guilt & Advice Between Friends* (Columbus, Ohio: HDC Press, 2014).

19 Miller McPherson, Lynn Smith-Lovin and Matthew E. Brashears, "Social Isolation in America: Changes in Core Discussion Networks over Two Decades," *American Sociological Review 2006*; 71; 353.

20 James A. Roberts, Ph.D. and Meredith David, Ph.D., "My Life has Become a Major Distraction from My Cell Phone: Partner Phubbing and Relationship Satisfaction among romantic partners," *Computers in Human Behavior,* Volume 54 (January 2016): 134-141.

21 David L. Strayer, Joel M. Cooper, Jonna Turrill, James R. Coleman, and Rachel J. Hopman, "Measuring Cognitive Distraction in the Automobile III: A Comparison of Ten 2015 In- Vehicle Information Systems," AAA Foundation for Public Safety, October 2015, accessed April 12, 2018, http://aaafoundation.org/wp-content/uploads/2017/12/MeasuringCognitiveDistractionintheAutomobileIIIReport.pdf.

22 Sean Coughlan. "Digital Dependence 'eroding Human Memory,'" *BBC News,* Oct 7, 2015, accessed April 12, 2018, http://www.bbc.com/news/education-34454264.

23 *The Wizard of Oz,* directed by Victor Fleming, George Cukor and Mervyn LeRoy (1939; United States; Metro Goldwyn Mayer Presents).

24 "Holmes-Rahe Stress Inventory," *The American Institute of Stress,* August 15, 2017, accessed April 12, 2018, http://www.stress.org/holmes-rahe-stress-inventory/.

25 J.T. Cacioppo & S. Cacioppo, "Social Relationships and Health: The Toxic Effects of Perceived Social Isolation," *Social and Personality Psychology Compass* 8, no. 2 (2014), doi:10.1111/spc3.12087.

26 Daniel Goleman, *Emotional Intelligence: Why It Can Matter More than IQ* (London: Bloomsbury, 2010).

27 Frederik Joelving, "Why the #$%! Do We Swear? For Pain Relief," *Scientific American,* July 12, 2009, accessed October 8, 2018, https://www.scientificamerican.com/article/why-do-we-swear/.

28 Bryan Gardiner, "Why Does Stubbing Your Toe Hurt So Damn Much?" *Wired,* June 06, 2017, accessed April 14, 2018, http://www.wired.com/2015/04/stubbing-toe-hurt-damn-much/.

29 Jon Ronson, *So You've Been Publicly Shamed* (New York: Riverhead Books, 2015).

30 "Ecotone," *The Encyclopedia of Earth*, last modified May 15, 2018, accessed October 8, 2018, https://editors.eol.org/eoearth/wiki/Ecotone.

31 Carolyn Keene, *Nancy Drew Mystery Stories* (New York: Grosset & Dunlap, 1930-1979). Print.

32 A. H. Maslow, "A Theory of Human Motivation," *Psychological Review* 50, no. 4 (1943), doi: 10.1037/h0054346.

33 "Laughter Yoga for Health and Happiness," Laughter Yoga University, accessed October 8, 2018, https://laughteryoga.org/laughter-yoga/about-laughter-yoga/.

34 Eleanor D. Payson, *The Wizard of Oz and Other Narcissists: Coping with the One-way Relationship in Work, Love, and Family* (Royal Oak, MI: Julian Day Publications, 2009). 17.

35 John Cacioppo and William Patrick, *Loneliness: Human Nature and the Need for Social Connection* (New York: W. W. Norton & Company, 2008). 71-72.

36 Vivian Giang, "How Smiling Changes Your Brain," *Fast Company*, January 30, 2015, ac- cessed April 14, 2018, https://www.fastcompany.com/3041438/how-smiling-changes-your-brain.

37 Aaron Smith and Monica Anderson, "Social Media Use 2018: Demographics and Statistics | Pew Research Center," Pew Research Center: Internet, Science & Tech, September 19, 2018, accessed October 07, 2018, http://www.pewinternet.org/2018/03/01/social-media-use-in-2018/.

38 J.D Vance, *Hillbilly Elegy: A Memoir of a Family and Culture in Crisis* (New York: Harper, 2018).

39 Piper Kerman, "Piper Kerman," (lecture, Upper Arlington Author Series, Upper Arlington, Ohio, December 1, 2016).